Soo Bahk

Volume 2

Len Losik Ph.D
5th Dan Black Belt

Soo Bahk

Ancient Ways, Modern Art

Volume 2

By

Len Losik Ph.D
5ᵗʰ *Dan Black Belt*

Soo Bahk

Ancient Ways, Modern Art

Volume 2

by
SanLen Publishing

Soo Bahk Ancient Ways Modern Art Volume 2. All rights are reserved. No part of this book may be reproduced or transmitted in any form, by any means, electronic or mechanical, including photocopying, recording or by any information storage and retrieval system without written permission from the author.

Disclaimer: Please note that the author and publisher of this book are NOT RESPONSIBLE in any way whatsoever for any injury that may result from learning, engaging or practicing the techniques of any of the styles and systems contained within, and/or following the recommendation and suggestions given. Since the physical activities referred to in this book may be too strenuous for some individuals to engage in safely, the author recommends consulting a physician prior to beginning training.

© Copyright March, 2003

First Printing 2003

ISBN 0-9661179-1-3

This book is dedicated to Great Grandmaster Hwang Kee in recognition of his life-long dedication and accomplishments in the Moo Duk Kwan

Great Grandmaster Founder of the Moo Duk Kwan, Hwang Kee

For their contribution to the accuracy and completeness of this book, I want to thank Master Dan Segarra and his assistant from the Soo Bahk Warrior-Scholar Academy for their review, suggestions and recommendations to improve this book's thoroughness and accuracy. I also want to thank Tang Soo Do Master Eric Madis for his review of this book and his many suggestions and recommendations he made for improvements to its accuracy and thoroughness.

CONTENTS

INTRODUCTION	15
THE HYUNG OF SOO BAHK DO	23
THE YUK RO HYUNG	27
THE CLASSICAL ANIMAL HYUNG	29
PYUNG AHN CHO DAN HYUNG	34
PYUNG AHN EE DAN HYUNG	39
PYUNG AHN SUM DAN HYUNG	45
PYUNG AHN SA DAN HYUNG	49
PYUNG AHN OH DAN HYUNG	56
NAI HANJI EE DAN HYUNG	62
NAI HANJI SUM DAN HYUNG	66
YUKRO CHO DAN	78
YUKRO EE DAN	85
YUK RO SUM DAN HYUNG	88
HWA SUNG HYUNG	99
BIBLIOGRAPHY	121
INDEX	131
BOOKS PUBLISHED BY THE AUTHOR	141

Introduction

Ancient Drawing Illustrating Korean Fighting Art

The ancient style of Soo Bahk was uncovered in 1957 by Moo Duk Kwan Tang Soo Do Grandmaster Hwang Kee. He found the book, *Moo Yei Tong Bo Ji* (military text with illustrations) at the Seoul railroad yard library where he worked. After studying, Grandmaster Hwang Kee translated a portion of the text and discovered that the region including Korea had an ancient martial art named Soo Bahk (Eng. Spelling) and it was more than 2000 years old

After translating more of the *Moo Yei Tong Bo Ji*, Grandmaster Hwang Kee created a series of new Hyungs that were inspired by the techniques Grandmaster Hwang Kee found in the *Moo Yei Do Bo Tong Ji*. He was so influenced by his discovery that he changed the name of his style from Tang Soo Do Moo Duk Kwan to the Tang Soo Do Moo Duk Kwan Soo Bahk®[1]. This new name recognized Soo Bahk as one of Korea's earliest centuries old, fighting styles.

At the same time, the post-war South Korean War government was working hard to establish its martial art styles as originating during the 5th century T'ang Dynasty or earlier and to apply to have its newly named martial art, Tae Kwon Do added to the Olympic games as Japan was doing for Judo, which was added in 1964 in the Tokyo games.

Grandmaster Hwang Kee wanted Tang Soo Do Moo Duk Kwan Soo Bahk to be a truly Korean expression and either Tang Soo Do or Soo Bahk recognized as the government sponsored martial art. Tae Kwon Do, Kwon Bup, Tae Kyun and Tang Soo Do are included in this book because for several decades the terms were used interchangeably to mean Korea's ancient fighting art

---

[1] Soo Bahk Do is a registered trademark of the U.S. Soo Bahk Do Moo Duk Kwan Federation, Springfield New Jersey

[2] Soo Bahk Doo Moo Duk Kwan is a registered trademark of the U.S. Soo Bahk Do Federation, Springfield New Jersey

depicted in regional cave murals and mountain temples. So, it is important to discuss these topics when discussing Soo Bahk Do.

The name Soo Bahk or possibly 'striking hand' was used centuries before, but the name Soo Bahk Do "the way of the hand and foot" was chosen by Moo Duk Kwan Tang Soo Do Grandmaster Hwang Kee in 1957. Thus, the discovery of the *Moo Yei Do Bo Tong Ji* gave great credence to those Koreans who said that Korea had once had her own fighting arts before the colonial Japanese occupation (circa 1874-1945). Today's Soo Bahk has evolved into a blend of modern Tang Soo Do, Chuan Fa and Okinawa Karate Do with a self-defense structure and teaching regimen taken from Okinawa Karate Do.

The Moo Duk Kwan Tang Soo Do Soo Bahk Do includes techniques from the centuries-old hand and foot fighting techniques described in the *Moo Yei Tong Bo Ji*, the techniques in the classical animal Hyungs practiced in the Okinawa martial arts, and, techniques from the Chinese Chuan Fa/Kwon Bup Hyung learned by Grandmaster Hwang Kee in his youth. The Kwon Bup Hyungs are the same Hyung used by the once powerful Korean forces from centuries before. Due to his loyalty to his native arts, Grandmaster Hwang Kee blended aspects of ancient Soo Bahk from the *Moo Yei Do Bo Tong Ji* with the more modern Moo Duk Kwan Tang Soo Do techniques and created the Moo Duk Kwan Tang Soo Do Soo Bahk Do®.

Starting in 1945, Koreans removed any ties to the decades-long Japanese occupation, and today the Moo Duk Kwan Tang Soo Do Soo Bahk Do® has become simply Moo Duk Kwan Soo Bahk Do®. Tang Soo Do is the Korean name for Okinawa and Japanese influenced Okinawa karate do. During the Japanese occupation, Okinawa karate do was considered Japanese since Japan invaded and converted the Okinawa culture to Japanese beginning in 1874. In 1995, the term Tang Soo Do was dropped as a symbol of World War II Korea.

The Moo Duk Kwan Soo Bahk Do is a 21st century martial art organization whose foundation includes the teachings of both ancient and modern martial arts/fighting arts masters. The name "Soo Bahk" or "striking hand" can be found in references as early as 2700 years ago from the age of Chun Chu, a member of the Chinese military. It could have been used even earlier, but there are few documents available to validate its use.

The term, Soo Bahk appears in the book, *Joa Jun* from the Han Dynasty in China some 2,000 years ago. Soo Bahk also appears in the book, *Han Seo* by the 10th King, Yae Je of the Han Dynasty. The breadth of Korea's influence expanded deep into areas of central China. Examples of Soo Bahk can be found in cave paintings and manuscripts left behind in several regions of China and in areas as far north as Manchuria.

Soo Bahk Do's modern techniques are from Tang Soo Do and include closed-hand techniques followed by advanced open-hand techniques.

Modern additions include closed and open hand techniques as upper body blocking, open and closed hand strikes, stepping, turning, ground level kicks, jump kicking, flying kicks, one step offensive movements with defensive countering, semi-free style and free style sparring, mind and body conditioning, Eastern philosophy, brick and board breaking, training in the classical animal Hyung as well as techniques inspired from the *Moo Yei Tong Bo*.

This includes training in the ancient Hyung as interpreted by Grandmaster Hwang Kee also from the *Moo Yei Do Bo Tong Ji*. These Hyung include the Chil Sung Hyung added in 1962, the Hwa Sun Hyung added in 1982, the Yuk Ro Hyung and the Ship Dan Kuem Hyung. The Ship (10) Dan (level) Kuem are taught only in Korea. The ancient techniques from the *Moo Yei Do Tong Bo Ji* were resurrected by Grandmaster Hwang Kee beginning in 1957 when he first discovered the *Moo Yei Do Bo Tong Ji* at the railroad library in Seoul.

Following WWII, Korea was struggling with understanding her history, no one, not even people working in the government remembered the martial arts community that had existed in Korea before the Japanese occupation. Grandmaster Hwang Kee immediately recognized the importance of the *Moo Yei Do Bo Tong Ji* to the existence of the newly resurrected Korean martial arts community. It was during this time that he translated several key symbols to mean Soo Bahk. Other symbols he translated to mean Kwon Bup (chuan fa or fist way).

These translations proved to Grandmaster Hwang Kee the existence of Korean martial arts from centuries before. Grandmaster In 1957 Grandmaster Hwang Kee began a life-long effort to resurrect Soo Bahk. As a direct consequence of this, there are many new Hyung and techniques in Soo Bahk Do® inspired by the *Moo Yei Do Bo Tong Ji*. Grand master Hwang Kee added a total of 23 new Hyung to Moo Duk Kwan Tang Soo Do after he resurrected Soo Bahk. These Hyung are inspired on the writings in the *Moo Yei Do Bo Tong Ji* as interpreted by Grandmaster Hwang Kee. These are now in the form of new Hyung which allows them to be learned and passed on to future practitioners.

SOO BAHK'S LINEAGE

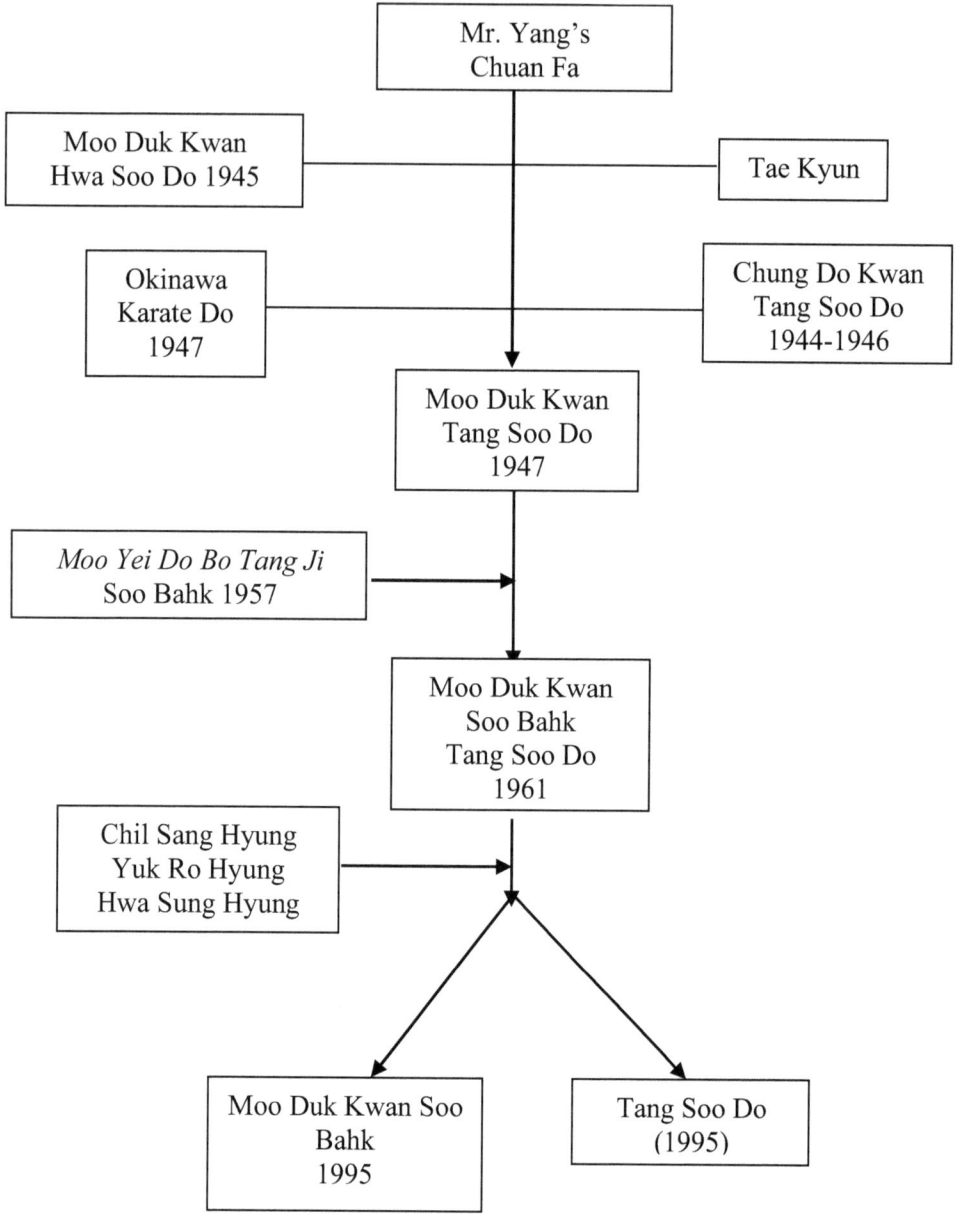

The Hyung of Soo Bahk Do

As Grandmaster Hwang Kee began his translation of the *Moo Yei Do Bo Tong Ji* in 1957, keeping the translation accurate was very important to him to avoid criticism. After much work, Grandmaster Hwang Kee translated the section on Kwon Bup in the *Moo Yei Do Bo Tong Ji*. Grandmaster Hwang Kee translated the Kwon Bup and many years, created and added a series of 23 new Hyung to the Moo Duk Kwan.

The first seven new Hyung were named Chil Sung, 10 other new Hyung he named Sip Dan Kuem and six other Hyung were named Yuk Ro referring to six pathways. The next Hyung he named Hwa Sun. for the seven stars in the Big Dipper stars in the northern sky.

Translating *the Moo Yei Do Tong Bo Ji* was very difficult because parts of the *Moo Yei Do Bo Tong Ji* were written in classical Chinese dialect that hasn't been used for 200 years. What makes translating ancient Chinese difficult is that all languages change with time and each character may have had several meanings, some of which are no longer known. This is similar to American English when the definition of a word has several meanings and its meaning depends on the context it is used.

The techniques recorded in the *Moo Yei Do Bo Tong Ji* were once known by the Emperor's armies. The techniques themselves build discipline, strength, speed and power, but the philosophical training in Soo Bahk Do® originates from the Moo Duk Kwan. Moo Duk Kwan can translate to "martial virtue institute." The philosophy of the Moo Duk Kwan combined with the physical challenges of Soo Bahk Do® creates a powerful way of training both mind and the body. This enables the practitioner to deal with the outside world in a mature, intelligent, forthright and virtuous manner.

There are three areas in Soo Bahk Do Moo Duk Kwan that are vital to the development of these qualities. These are the Neh Gong, Weh Gong and Shim Gong. Neh Gong, or internal exercises that improve one's internal health and energy. Weh Gong, for external exercises, improves one's physical health, muscles, tendons, etc. Shim Gong for spiritual development, improves one's mental and spiritual health and overall well-being.

The integration of these areas of development through the mental and physical challenges of the Chil Sung, Yuk Ro, Hwa Sung Ship Dan Kyum training, and the Moo Duk Kwan's own philosophy guides the practitioner towards a oneness with their environment whether it's physical, spiritual or social, creating a more calm and peaceful practitioner, and a peaceful and calm surrounding.

When master Lee Duk Moo compiled the *Moo Yei Do Bo Tong Ji* he probably did not ponder the world-wide importance it would have, let alone its use toward human betterment in our present time. This ancient text has stood the test of time and has survived antiquity to remind us of the heritage of the ancient warriors of Korea. These efforts and sacrifices helped to pass on to us the values of Soo Bahk Do® and the traditional martial arts of Korea.

Once a student nears Dan level in Soo Bahk Do® Moo Duk Kwan he/she learns advanced Hyung including the classical animal Hyung. The Korean people have attached animal traits to these Hyung that assist in illustrating the character of the Hyung. These symbols include the bear, cobra, crane, heron, eagle, swallow, ram and the tiger. Each of these helps the practitioner continue to hone their skills.

The Kee Cho Hyung

The Kee Cho Hyung appeared very early in the Moo Duk Kwan's history. They were incorporated in Tang Soo Do in 1947. The

Kee Cho Hyungs are considered the "foundation Hyungs". The Kee Cho Hyungs are the first three of many learned in Soo Bahk Do® Moo Duk Kwan.

The Kee Cho (Hwang Kee's lessor) Hyung are a series of three Hyung, each made up of basic blocks, punches, strikes, stances and stepping and turning movements for developing one's balance, coordination, breathing and hand-eye-foot coordination. Kee Cho Hyung can translate to "Hwang Kee's lesser Hyung" being lessor to the Pyung Ahn Hyungs.

A high level of physical coordination and balance is needed in the next level of Hyung that are the intermediate to Kee Cho Hyung were created and added for the new student to provide a series of Hyung slightly less challenging than the Pyung Ahn Hyung series.

The Kee Cho Hyung in Soo Bahk Do® are as tools to expose the fundamental skills needed to continue on in training learning more complex Hyung that contain the techniques of self-defense. This is in a similar manner that a child must first learn to stand up and take its first steps to later, learn to run.

The Pyung Ahn Hyung

The Pyung Ahn Hyung series were based on Okinawa Hyung called the Pinan Kata, which first created by the Okinawa karate master Itosu Yatsusune in Okinawa. master Itosu took the classical Chinese Hyung, Kushanku (Kong Sang Koon) and created five new Hyung and named them Pinan (Kor. Pyung Ahn).

The classical Kong Sang Koon Hyung is named for a traveling Chinese official believed to have been proficient in the White Crane Fist style of Chuan Fa. He visited Okinawa on a regular basis during the 18th century. During his stay, he taught the Hyung to interested Okinawa practitioners who later named this
Hyung in his honor.

The Pyung Ahn Hyung were originally developed for school children instead teaching children Hyungs like Nai Hanji and Bassai. The classical Hyung such as Nai Hanji, Ship Sam, Jion, Tjin, etc. were held in high regard, at the turn of the 20th century. to teach them to children was disrespectful. The Pyung Ahn series are lesser level Hyung to the Nai Hanji series. This can be seen in the name of the first one, Pyung Ahn Cho Dan or "lesser level of the Pyung Ahn Hyung".

A clearer name for each one in the series would be Pyung Ahn Cho Il Dan Hyung. Pyung Ahn Cho Ee Dan Hyung, Pyung Ahn Cho Sam Dan Hyung and Pyung Ahn Cho Sa Dan Hyung and Pyung Ahn Cho O Dan Hyung. Before the Pyung Ahn Hyung, the Hyung were learned only by adults. Master Ankoh Itosu taught elementary grade school in the Okinawa schools and in 1905, Master Itosu began teaching the Pinan series of Kata he created to his school children likely using the Kusanku (Kong Sang Koon) Kata for the techniques.

The Pinan Kata were utilized by Funakoshi Gichin in Japan in his karate do schools. Funakoshi renamed them the Japanese term. In Soo Bahk Do®, the philosophy behind teaching the Pyung Ahn Hyung is to add more self-defense techniques to a new student's experience, improve the practitioner's proficiency, develop more discipline, improve breathing, balance and quickness of movements needed for learning the next level Hyung. Learning the Pyung Ahn series improves the practitioner's self-confidence and at the same time, improves their inner peace.

The Pyung Ahn Hyungs has the symbol of the turtle associated with them. The Pyung Ahn are the first series of Korean Hyung to have an animal symbol. The turtle is used to identify the characteristics one will develop by learning the Pyung Ahn Hyung effectively. The turtle appears to be calm and patient just like the practitioners after learning the Pyung Ahn Hyung series.

The turtle appears to be weaponless, but it is protected by an almost indestructible shell. It has incredibly sharp and powerful jaw, claws and legs that take the turtle around the world one stroke at a time, and a jaw of incredible power. The turtle is found everywhere in the world and travels great distances using its incredible stamina. As a symbol in Korean culture, the turtle is known for many good qualities including wisdom, patience, longevity and peace.

The Chil Sung Hyung

The name Chil Sung Hyung comes from the *Moo Yei Do Bo Tong Ji*. The Chil Sung Hyung were developed and added to Moo Duk Kwan Tang Soo Do by Grandmaster Hwang Kee in 1962 and are inspired by the movements in the *Moo Yei Do Bo Tong Ji*.

Chil Sung Hyungs are a series of seven Hyung soft and hard blocking, kicking, striking and self-defense techniques indigenous to the region similar to those in the Hyung of Kwon Bup. Learning the Chil Sung Hyung gives techniques to avoid clinching and wrestling and to gain the advantage by using the opponent's own actions and reactions when breaking holds using the seven stars, e.g., the head, shoulder, elbow, hand, hip, knee, and foot. Chil means 'seven' and Sung means 'stars'.

The term comes from the Taoist recognition of the seven stars of the Big Dipper constellation of stars in the northern sky. The Big Dipper is used by travelers to locate the North star in the constellation Ursa Major, thus the north direction. The two stars on the outside edge of the big dipper cup point directly at the North Star. Once the North Star is located, a traveler can determine east, west and south directions and arrive at their destination by using the setting and rising of the sun for east and west along with the direction of true north.

Although the Big Dipper is not a formal constellation, the picture of the Big Dipper shows you a very noticeable seven stars of the "Big Dipper" constellation. The stars form the lower part of the body and tail of the true constellation, the "Big Bear", Ursa Major. The Big Dipper is very famous as a "polestar finder", we can find the north star, Polaris by stretching a line of two stars at the tip of dipper. The star labeled Mizar, the second star from the tip of handle, is a well-known double star with a 5th magnitude star named "Alcor", detectable with naked eyes.

The Big Dipper can be found very easily in northern sky by all of the northern continents, so it has been connected with various customs all over the ancient world. In China, they saw the Big Dipper as an ox-drawn carriage of the Emperor, American Indians regarded it as a big bear, the same with the ancient Greeks. In case of Japan, though "*Hokuto-shichisei* (the northern seven stars of dipper)" is most general, there were other names loke "the stars of seven-week days" or "the stars of rudder", etc.

The learning of the Chil Sung Hyung or seven stars, also helps to orient us on our path to greater wisdom and understanding like a child learning their first steps as in the Kee Cho Hyung. They also develop feeling peaceful and self-confident as in learning the Pyung Ahn Hyung series. They serve as a guide to responding to the world around us. In learning the Chil Sung Hyung we react more and more with maturity in both action and thought.

The Yuk Ro Hyung

In 1790, master Lee Duk Moo appeared before King Jung Jo and was ordered to compile Korea's martial arts techniques that were popular at that time into a book. master Lee Duk Moo referenced many sources all of which are listed in the *Moo Yei Do Bo Tong Ji's* contents.

The *Moo Yei Do Bo Tong Ji* was written in four parts or sections. Section I was written about the spear (Chang) techniques, their various types and offensive and defensive techniques. Section II describes the sword (Kuem) techniques. Section III describes the long-bladed sword techniques and sword strategies and Section IV is about empty hand combat (Kwon Bup) techniques.

The Kwon Bup section describes the most effective techniques for empty hand combat that were known up to the time. These were interpreted by Grandmaster Hwang Kee and he created the seven Yuk Ro Hyung from them. Practicing these techniques in the Yuk Ro which means the "six paths". These Hyung are said to make the practitioner's bones extra hard. One application for having hard bones is to be able to inflict great injury on an adversary while also having powerful defensive technique. The name, Yuk Ro name comes from the *Moo Yei Do Bo Tong Ji*. Yukro, which means "6 paths" and are meant to strengthen a practitioner's bones and make them very hard for sustaining very little injury in the event of an attack and then inflicting greater injury to an adversary in battle. The six paths refer to the six paths to enlightenment.

These are also referred to as the six paths of rebirth or six destinies and are part of the Ten Dharma Realms in Confucius teaching. The six paths of rebirth include the six principles of the Ten Thousand Buddhas and are 1) do not take a life without purpose 2) have no greed 3) be content 4) have no selfishness 5) do not seek personal gain and 6) do not lie.

Ship Dan Kuem Hyung

The name, Ship Dan Kuen comes from the *Moo Yei Do Bo Tong Ji*. The application of the techniques of the Ship Dan Kum (10 levels) Hyung are to inflict great injury on an adversary after some period of time, as in a delayed reaction. These Hyung are taught primarily in Korea. They consist of both hard and soft techniques blended together to be both smooth and flowing.

The Sip Dan Kuem or ten levels of difficulty were created by Grandmaster Hwang Kee and inspired from techniques in the *Moo Yei Do Bo Tong Ji*. The techniques in the Sip Dan Kuem include hard and soft techniques and are believed to inflict great injury after some period of time of being hit.

Hwa Sun Hyung

The Hwa Sun Hyung was created using the techniques illustrated in the *Moo Yei Do Bo Tong Ji* and consists of both soft and hard techniques as well as advanced stances as well as powerful punching and blocking techniques.

The Hwa Sun Hyung was created by Grandmaster Hwang Kee inspired from the *Moo Yei Do Bo Tong Ji*. The Hwa Sun Hyung or "Hyung of the pure flower" was added to Soo Bahk Do® in 1982. Grandmaster Hwang Kee demonstrated the Hwa Sun Hyung personally for the first time in 1982. The Hwa Sun Hyung is the highest level Hyung in Soo Bahk Do® and contains more than 100 movements.

The Classical Animal Hyung

The classical Hyung are well over 300 hundred years old. Many animal symbols are associated with these Hyung. Most originated in China during the Tang Dynasty and were incorporated into the many styles of Chuan Fa in existence in central China.

They were eventually brought to Okinawa by Chinese travelers over the centuries and modified by Okinawa practitioners in the 19th and 20th century. They were brought to Korea at the end of the 19th century through the middle of the 20th century by both Japanese and Okinawa Instructors. The concept of using animal movements and physical characteristics in self-defense dates back to the 6th century when nature was greatly revered. Consequently, the Chinese evolved methods of fighting based on the movements of animals.

The Five Element system, a descendent of the Xin Yi Liu He Quan system from central China originating during the Sung Dynasty, known originally as the Xing Yi Quan, may be the source of many of today's classical animal Hyung. The movements of the Five Element system Hyung are linear, the practitioner moves through the Hyung coordinating all aspects of their bodies into focused strikes.

There are few kicks in these Hyung, emphasis is placed on generating great striking power using the entire body as the source of energy. After a certain level is acquired, the student moves onto the 12 animal Hyung. The 12 animal Hyung movements are variations of the Five Element system. The Hyung from the Twelve Animal system are based on the spirit of real and mythical animals including the dragon, crane, tiger, hawk, snake, mantis, bear, eagle and swallow. Many of these are also animal symbols used in the Chinese calendar and other astrological and cultural areas.

Each animal Hyung is used to illustrate to a student both the physical concepts behind each animal's physical movements and internal aspects too. These animal Hyungs migrated east to Okinawa and north to Korea. The animal concepts form the basis of the Okinawa karate do system created in the 17th century and the Japanese karate systems from the 1930's. They have been a mainstay of Moo Duk Kwan Tang Soo Do Soo Bahk Do® for many decades.

The classical Hyung include the Nai Hanji Hyung from the Okinawa city of Na Ha which uses the bear (for great power) as its symbol; Bassai is often translated to mean to break through barriers.

Hyungs which use the cobra (for quick, silent, striking blows) as it's symbol, Ship Sum which uses the Praying Mantis for its lightning quick death strikes, the Ginto Hyung which uses the crane (for sharp, quick strikes) as it's symbol, Ship Soo (ten hands, from the twelve hands Chuan Fa system) which uses the sparrow (quick, deceptive strikes) as it's symbol, Jion (from the temple grounds) which uses the ram (for generating incredible powerful strikes) as it's symbol, Wang Shu which uses the swallow (for blinding speed) as it's symbol, Kong Sang Koon which uses the eagle (for the powerful simultaneous hand and foot strikes) as it's symbol,

Sojin which uses the bull (powerful overpowering techniques) as its symbol and O Sip Sa Bo which uses the tiger (unstoppable, silent power) for its symbol. In 1957 Grandmaster Hwang Kee began a long-term effort to resurrect Soo Bahk Do®. As a direct consequence of this, there are more Soo Bahk Do® techniques than ever inspired by the *Moo Yei Do Bo Tong Ji*. Grandmaster Hwang Kee added many new Hyung to Moo Duk Kwan Tang Soo Do when he resurrected Soo Bahk.

These are based almost completely on the writing in the *Moo Yei Do Bo Tong Ji* as interpreted by Grandmaster Hwang Kee. These are now in the form of new Hyung that allows them to be learned and passed down to future practitioners. In the year 2001, Soo Bahk Do® Moo Duk Kwan will only be 34 years old. While other styles have changed their focus, Soo Bahk Do® Moo Duk Kwan remains staunchly focused on traditional facets of the physical and philosophical training. Soo Bahk Do® is well connected to Korea's many ancient fighting systems and their contribution to modern martial arts.

The future for Moo Duk Kwan Soo Bahk Do® may include increasing more of the Korean aspects while removing others. With all the Hyung from both Tang Soo Do and Soo Bahk Do® available, it is likely that the importance of the Tang Soo Do Hyung will lessen and the importance of the Chil Sang, Yuk Ro and Hwa Sun Hyung will increase.

HYUNG TO KATA CONVERSION MATRIX

KOREAN	JAPANESE	OKINAWA	SYMBOL
Passae (2)	Bassai (2)	Passai (2)	Cobra
Nai Hanji (3)	Tekki (3)	Nai Fanji (3)	Bear
Sip Sum	Hangetsu	Seisan	Preying Mantis
Jion	Jion	Jion	Goat
Tjin	Jion	Jion Ji	Goat
Chinto	Gankaku	Chinto	Crane
Sip Soo	Jutte	Jutte	Staff
Wangshu	Empi	Wanshu	Swallow
Kang Sang Koon (2)	Kanku (2)	Kusanku (2)	Eagle
O Sip Sa Bo (2)	Gojushiho (2)	Useishi (2)	Tiger
Woon Su	Un Su	Un Su	Heron
Rohee/Lohi (3)	Rohai (3)	Rohai (3)	Crane
Sojin	Sochin	Sochin	Bull

Soo Bahk Do Hyungs
(circa 1995)

The Pyung Ahn Hyungs – The Hyungs that Develop Self-Confidence.

      1. Pyung Ahn Cho Dan – The First of the Lesser Hyung

      2. Pyung Ahn Ee Dan - The Second of the Lesser Hyung

      3. Pyung Ahn Sum Dan - The Third of the Lesser Hyung

      4. Pyung Ahn Sa Dan – The Forth of the Lesser Hyung

      5. Pyung Ahn O Dan - The Fifth of the Lesser Hyung

Nai Hanji Hyungs – Hyungs from the City of Na Ha, Okinawa

      1. Nai Hanji E Dan – Second of the Lesser Nai Hanji Hyung
      2. Nai Hanji Sum Dan – Third of the Lesser Nai Hanji Hyung

Yuk Ro Hyungs – The Hyungs of the Six Paths

      1. Yuk Ro Il Ro – The First of the Sixth Paths Hyung

      2. Yuk Ro E Ro – The Second of the Sixth Paths Hyung

      3. Yuk Ro Sum Ro – The Third of the Sixth Paths Hyung

Hwa Sun Hyung – Hyung of the purest flower

      Hwa Sun

Pyung Ahn Cho Dan Hyung

PYUNG AHN CHO DAN

Chun Bee

1. Turn 90 degrees to the left, forward stance, low block with left hand.
2. Lunge punch with right fist to the face.
3. Turn 180 degrees to the right, forward stance, low block with right fist.
4. Pull right fist back, back stance, hammer fist strike, right foot back to left foot at heels.
5. Lunge punch with left fist to the solar plexus.
6. Turn 90 degrees to the left, left foot forward, forward stance, low block with left fist, middle soo do with left knife hand, right fist remain at right hip.
7. Step forward with right foot, upper block with right fist- pause.
8. Step forward with left foot, upper block with left fist.
9. Step forward with right foot, upper block with right fist-kia
10. Turn 270 degrees to the left, low block with left hand forward stance.
11. Lunge punch with right fist.
12. Turn 180 degrees to the right, low block with right fist.
13. Lunge punch with left fist.
14. Turn 90 degrees to the left, low block with left fist.
15. Lunge punch with right fist-pause.
16. Lunge punch with left fist.
17. Lunge punch with right fist-kia
18. Turn 270 degrees to the left, lower knife hand soo do, back stance with heel off ground, left foot forward.
19. Step off 45 degrees to the right, lower knife hand soo do, back stance with heel off the ground.
20. Turn 180 degrees to the right, lower knife hand soo do, back stance with front heel off the ground, right foot forward.
21. Step off 45 degrees to the left, lower knife hand soo do, back stance with front heel off the ground, left foot forward.

Chun Bee

PYUNG AHN CHO DAN

Pyung Ahn Ee Dan Hyung

PYUNG AHN EE DAN

Chun Bee

1. Turn 90 degrees to the left, left fist on top of right fist at right side, back stance, left foot forward, right arm to upper block position, left fist to inside out block with fist turned 90 degrees clockwise, hook punch with right fist to left side, left fist to left side
2. Side thrust punch shoulder high with left fist, right fist to right side, horse stance
3. Turn 180 degrees to the right, right fist on top of left fist at left side, back stance, right foot forward, left arm to upper block position, right fist to inside out block with fist turned 90 degrees clockwise, hook punch with left fist to right side, right fist to right side
4. Side thrust punch shoulder high with right fist, left fist to left side, horse stance
5. Left foot to right, right fist on top of left fist on left side, right foot to left knee to side kick position
6. Side kick with right foot, simultaneous chop with right soo do, cover for middle soo do, turn 180 degrees to the left, middle soo do, back stance with left foot forward
7. Step forward with right foot, back stance, middle soo do
8. Step forward with left foot, back stance, middle soo do
9. Step forward with right foot, forward stance, cover with left hand, spear hand thrust to solar plexus-kia
1. I0. Turn 270 degrees to the left, back stance, left foot forward, middle soo do
10. Step forward 45 degrees to the right with the right foot forward, middle soo do, back stance
11. Turn 135 degrees to the right, back stance, right foot forward, middle soo do
12. Step forward 45 degrees to the left with the left foot forward, middle soo do, back stance
13. Step with the left foot 105 degrees to the left, left arm cross from right to left at lower abdominal level, palm hand open, sweeping, right arm follows left for inside out block
14. Front snap kick with right foot, reverse punch with left fist, inside out block with left fist, modified forward stance, 30c) off from rear line
15. Front snap kick with left foot, reverse punch with right fist, inside out block with right fist, forward stance

16. Step forward with right foot, bring right fist on top of left fist to left side, back stance, then pivot to forward stance, re-enforced forearm block with right fist-kia
17. Turn 270 degrees to the left, forward stance, left foot forward, low block with left fist, cover to the right 45 degrees with high knife hand soo do
18. Step forward 45 degree to the right with right foot into forward stance, upper block
19. Turn 135 degrees to the right, forward stance, right foot forward, low block with right fist, cover to the left 45 degrees with high knife hand soo do
20. Step forward 45 degree to the left with left foot into forward stance, upper block

Chun Bee

PYUNG AHN EE DAN

Pyung Ahn Sum Dan Hyung

PYUNG AHN SUM DAN

Chun Bee

1. Turn 90 degrees to the left, inside out block with left fist, back stance, left foot forward
2. Right foot to left foot, knees bent, punch to groin level with right fist, punch to groin level with left fist, inside up punch with right fist, punch to the groin with right fist, inside up punch with left fist
3. Turn 180 degrees to the right, inside out block with right fist back stance
4. Left foot to right foot, knees bent, punch to the groin with left fist, punch to groin level with right fist, inside up punch with left fist, punch to the groin with left fist, inside up punch with left fist, left fist on top of right fist, on right hip
5. Turn 90 degrees to the left, left foot forward, back stance, re-enforced forearm block with left fist
6. Step forward with right foot, forward stance, spear hand thrust with right hand to solar plexus, cover with left palm hand to below right elbow
7. Turn 180 degrees to the left into horse stance, tuck right palm hand to right side with back of hand to side, horizontal hammer fist strike with left fist, horse stance, right fist to right hip, punching position
8. Pivot 90 degrees to the left, lunge punch with right fist-kia
9. Turn 180 degrees to the left, hooking with left foot at beginning of turn, knuckles to the hips
10. Crescent kick with right foot, land in horse stance, rotate upper body for right elbow deflection, hammer fist strike with right fist, return right fist knuckles to right hip
11. Crescent kick with left foot, land in horse stance, rotate upper body for left elbow deflection, hammer fist strike with left fist, return left fist knuckles to left hip
12. Crescent kick with right foot, land **in** horse stance, rotate upper body for right elbow deflection, hammer fist strike with right fist, right elbow to right side, inside out block position, left fist to punching position **on** left hip
13. Pivot 90 degrees to the right, lunge punch with left fist, left foot forward-kia
14. Right foot to left foot to horse stance, turn 1800 strike with right fist to left side of head for hook punch, simultaneous elbow strike with left elbow
15. Shuffle to the right for hook punch with left fist to right side of head, simultaneous elbow strike with right elbow

Chun Bee

PYUNG AHN SUM DAN

21b

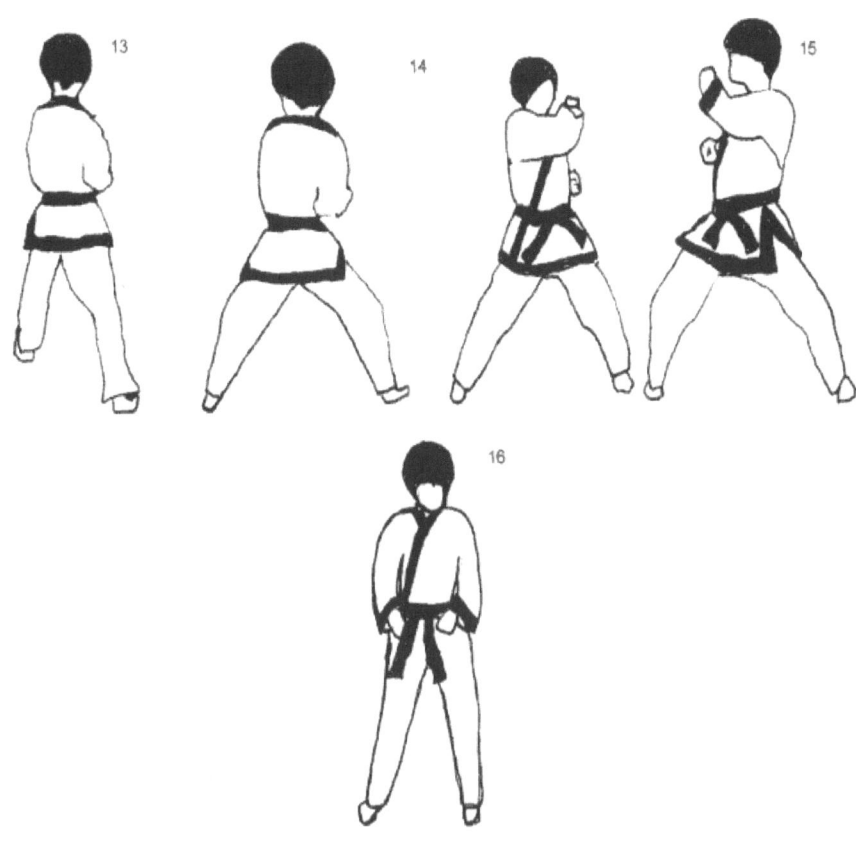

Pyung Ahn Sa Dan Hyung

PYUNG AHN SA DAN

Chun Bee

1. Turn 90 degrees to the left, left fist on top of right fist, on right hip, back stance, upper knife hand block with right knife hand, back of the hand inside out block with left knife hand-dynamic breathing during blocking
2. Turn 180 degrees to the right, right fist on top of left fist, on left hip, back stance, upper knife hand block with left knife hand, back of the hand inside out block with right knife hand-dynamic breathing during blocking
3. Turn 90 degrees to the left, left fist on top of right fist on right hip, back stance, low cross arm block, forward stance
4. Step forward with right foot, re-enforced forearm block with right arm, back stance, left fist on top of right fist on right hip, left knee up, bottom of foot parallel to floor
5. Side kick with left foot, simultaneous back fist strike with left fist, land in horse stance, elbow smash with right elbow into left palm hand, right fist on top of left fist on left hip, left foot to right foot
6. Side kick with right foot, simultaneous back fist strike with right fist, land in horse stance, elbow smash with left elbow into right palm hand, forward stance with right foot forward
7. Pivot to the left into forward stance, left knife hand cover to the left side of knee, palm toward knee, right knife hand to upper knife hand block, pivot on balls of feet 90 degrees to the left, chop with right knife hand, cover to the left side of head with left knife hand, back of hand to inside facing head
8. Front snap kick with right foot, step forward with left foot behind right foot, right knife hand goes low into circular vertical back fist strike, left hand covers over right hand in circular motion during the step forward motion, left fist to left side-kia
9. Turn 225 degrees to the left, forward stance, high cross arm block at neck level with knife hand, right hand over left, close fist, pull both fists down to chest level, rotate right fist 90 degrees clockwise
10. Pull back right fist to right side simultaneous front snap kick with right leg, land in forward stance, right leg forward, reverse punch with left fist, punch with right fist
11. Turn 90 degrees to the right into forward stance, right leg forward, high cross arm block at neck level with knife hand, right hand over left, close fist, pull both fists down to chest level, rotate right fist 90 degrees clockwise

12. Pull back left fist to left side simultaneous front snap kick with left leg, land in forward stance, left leg forward, reverse punch with right fist, punch with left fist
13. Turn 45 degrees with left leg forward, re-enforced forearm block with left arm, back stance
14. Step forward with right foot into back stance, re-enforced forearm block with the right arm
15. Step forward with left foot into back stance, re-enforced forearm block with the left arm
16. Pivot into forward stance, left foot forward, grab with open palm hands to neck level, head smash closing fists during smash-kia
17. Turn 225 degrees to the left, middle soo do, back stance, left foot forward
18. Turn 90 degrees to the right, middle soo do, back stance, right foot forward

Chun Bee

PYUNG AHN SA DAN

Pyung Ahn Oh Dan Hyung

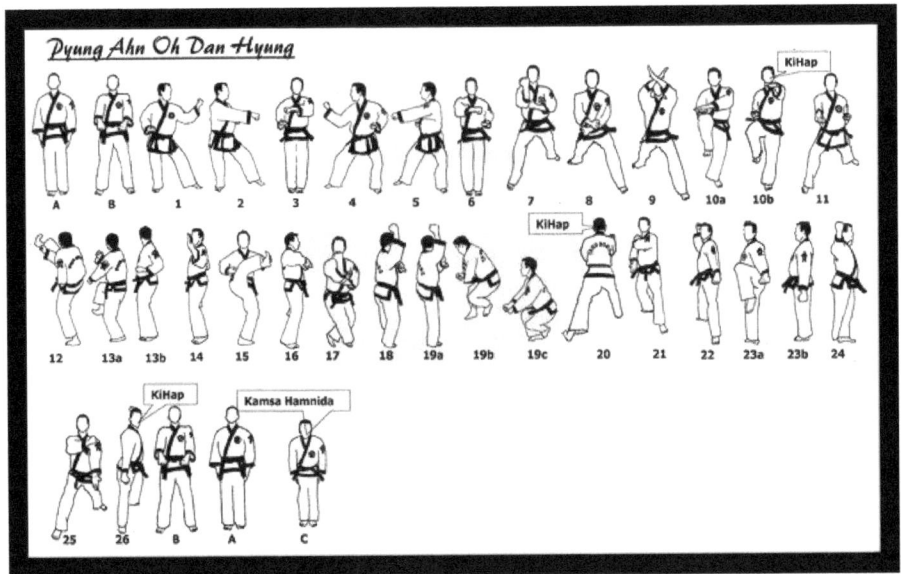

PYUNG AHN O DAN

Chun Bee

1. Turn to the left 90 degrees, inside-out block with left fist, back stance, hook punch with right fist, solar plexus level
2. Bring left foot back to right foot, facing beginning direction, left fist on top of right fist on right side
3. Turn to the right 90 degrees, inside-out block, back stance, hook punch with left fist, solar plexus level
4. Bring right foot back to left foot, facing beginning direction, right fist on top of left fist on left side
5. Step forward with right foot, re-enforced forearm block with right arm, back stance
6. Step forward with left foot, forward stance, low cross-arm block, quickly pull fists back to right hip, back stance, high cross-arm block, front stance, knife hand, rotate left hand under right, pivoting at wrist, until left hand is on top, draw both hands back to chest level, chop to neck level with left knife hand, draw right fist back to right hip,
7. Step forward lunge punch with right fist
8. Turning 180 degrees to the left, crescent kick with right foot, low block with right fist, horse stance, left fist to left hip, arms parallel at chest level. Chop to the left with left knife hand, right fist to right side, rotate left knife hand 90 degrees counter clock-wise to vertical position, pivot to the left on balls of feet 90 degrees
9. Crescent kick with right foot into open left palm hand, follow with elbow smash with right elbow into open left palm hand
10. Step with left foot to behind right foot, back-fist strike with right arm in vertical position, left fist to right elbow vertical strike with right fist, open left fist to cover under arm area
11. Left foot forward to modified back stance, right fist knuckles to right hip, left fist knuckles to left hip
12. Stepping forward with right foot, leap into the air turn 90 degrees to the left, tucking feet under bottom, land with left foot behind right foot, land with knees bent low, low cross-arm block
13. Turn to the right 90 degrees, step forward into forward stance with right foot, re-enforced forearm block with right fist-kia
14. Vertical hammer fist downward with left fist on the left side, pull left knee up simultaneously, right fist to right side
15. Turn 180 degrees to the left, spear hand thrust with right hand, cover with left open palm hand to neck, forward stance with left foot forward, pull back-to-back stance, right arm to vertical block, left fist to low block, pause
16. Left foot to right foot, pivot 180 degrees to the left on balls of feet, right foot behind left foot, palm hands cover low groin area, left hand

over right hand, pull both hands up keeping hands together while rotating for vertical break, pulling arms apart at chest level for break away
17. Step forward with right foot, spear hand thrust with left hand, cover with right open palm hand to neck, forward stance with right foot forward, pull spear hand back to vertical block, right fist to low block into back stance
18. Step back with right foot to left, right fist over left fist at low stomach level while
19. Right foot is brought back to left foot

Chun Bee

PYUNG AHN O DAN

Nai Hanji Ee Dan Hyung

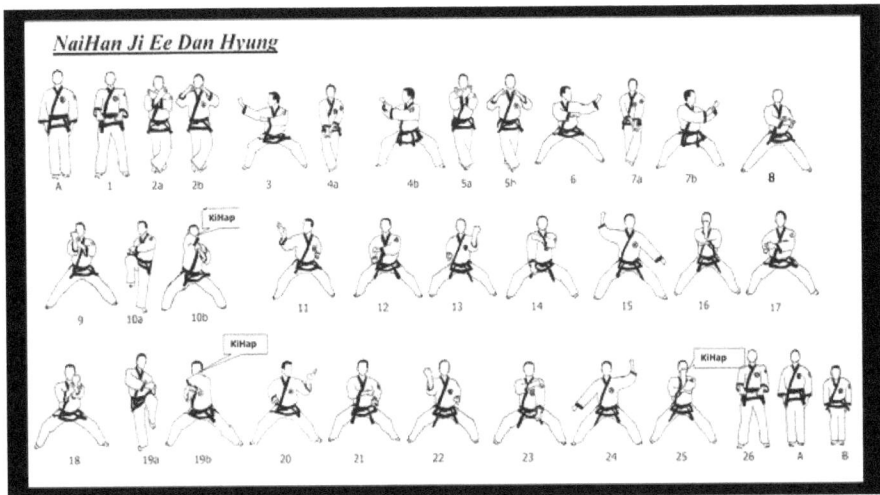

NAI HANJI EE DAN

Chun Bee

1. Cross left foot in front of right foot, left arm in front of right arm for a high open-handed cross block over the head, pull arms down to high vertical block position, forearms sent 450, palms of the hand toward side of head
2. Inside-out crescent with right leg, double fisted strike parallel to ground, strike and stomp with right foot simultaneously
3. Grab right fist with left hand, pull back right fist with left hand all the way to chest and push right fist back to striking position as left foot crosses right foot, step out in horse stance
4. Cross right foot over left foot, cross left hand over right hand for a high open-handed gross block over the head, pull arms down to vertical block position, forearms bent 450
5. Inside-out crescent with left leg, double fisted strike parallel to ground, strike and stomp with left foot simultaneously
6. Grab left fist with right hand, pull back left fist with right hand all the way to chest and push left fist back to striking position as right foot crosses left foot, step into horse stance, left fist to left hip, right palm hand to front of left fist, inside out block with right fist, slide left palm hand to right wrist during block, draw right fist with left palm hand to right side,
7. Raise right knee to waist level, land in horse stance, elbow smash with right elbow, chop with right soo do, hook punch with left fist
8. Cross left foot over right foot, crescent kick with right foot, step into horse stance, back fist strike with left fist-kia, low punch with right fist, left palm hand cover at right elbow,
9. Draw right fist back to high vertical position, left fist to low cover at waste level, back fist strike with right fist to face height, left fist to below right elbow, right fist to right side, cover right fist with left palm hand, inside block with left fist,
10. Slide right hand to left wrist. Draw left fist to left side, cover left fist with right hand
11. Draw left knee up to waist level, elbow smash with left elbow, horse stance, chop with left soo do, hook punch with right fist
12. Cross right foot over left foot, crescent kick with left foot, land in horse stance, back fist strike with right fist-kia, low punch with left fist, right palm hand cover at left elbow, draw left fist to high vertical position, right fist cover low at waste level, back fist strike with left fist to face level, right fist to left elbow-kia

Chun Bee

NAI HANJI EE DAN

Nai Hanji Sum Dan Hyung

NAI HANJI SUM DAN

Chun Bee

1. Inside block with left hand, right fist back to right side, horse stance, drive right fist down to groin level, inside block with right fist, left fist to left side, horse stance, right fist to left side of head, back fist strike with right fist, right fist to right side, fore arm parallel to ground, vertical arm position, right fist back fist strike, horse stance, reverse punch with right fist, horse stance, draw right fist back to right side, slide left hand to right wrist
2. Simultaneously, rotate right arm outward to right side, pushing right fist out with left hand, and step with left foot over right, land in horse stance as right wrist and left hand are rotated clock-wise in large circle, punch with right fist, keep left hand on upper forearm, inside-out block with right fist,
3. Low block with left fist, rotate right arm over left arm close to chest, draw left fist up to left vertical striking position, right hand cover with close fist, back fist strike with left fist, move right fist to below left elbow at strike
4. Draw left fist across to right shoulder, back fist strike with left hand, cross right foot over left foot, land in horse stance, keep right fist under left elbow, draw left fist to high vertical striking position on left side, horse stance, back fist strike with left fist-kia, left fist to left side, keep right hand on left fist, horse stance, punch with left fist, right hand on top of left arm, draw back left fist to left side, keep right hand on left fist
5. Right foot over left foot, push left fist away from body with right hand, land in horse stance, rotate left fist in large counter clock-wise circle back to side position, punch with left fist, keep right hand on top of left arm, knife hand chop with right hand, left fist back to left side, hook punch with left fist, right hand to right side
6. Cross left foot over right foot, inside out crescent kick with right foot, land in horse stance, back fist strike with left hand at waste level-kia

Chun Bee

NAI HANJI SUM DAN

YUKRO CHO DAN HYUNG

Chun Bee

1. Left foot to right foot, extend right arm straight out. Right arm parallel to the ground, right palm fist facing body, look straight ahead.
2. Lift left foot into left leg forward stance, simultaneously extend both arms straight out away from body, left fist in front of left knee and higher, right fist over right leg.
3. Rotate waist and upper body 180° to the left side.
4. Extend the left arm out to the right arm, grasp right hand's fingers at chin height.
5. Draw back into back stance left foot forward knee locked, making a scooping motion and bring both hands to lower abdomen level, palm over back of the hand, palms facing downward. While moving forward into a forward stance with left foot forward, draw both open hands up to chest level, and then exhaling slowing push both palm hands out to full arm extension.
6. Bring both palm hands back to hips, inhaling slowly, shift weight to back right leg, draw back into back stance left foot forward knee locked,
7. While moving forward into a forward stance with left foot forward, draw both open hands up to chest level, and then exhaling slowing push both palm hands out to full arm extension.
8. Draw right hand back to right hip, while pressing down with extended left palm hand, execute right leg front low thrust kick with toes pointed out to the right.
9. Land in right foot forward stance, extend right fist out over right knee at chest level, extend left fist over left knee at chest height.
10. Rotate upper body and arms 180° to the right, keeping fist at same level.
11. Extend the right arm out to the left arm, grasp left hand's fingers at chin height.
12. Draw back into back stance right foot forward right knee locked, making a scooping motion and bring both hands to lower abdomen level, palm over back of the hand, palms facing downward. While moving forward into a forward stance with right foot forward, draw both open hands up to chest level, and then exhaling slowing push both palm hands out to full arm extension.
13. Draw back into back stance right foot forward right knee locked, making a scooping motion and bring both hands to hips.
14. While moving forward into a forward stance with right foot forward, draw both open hands up to chest level, and then exhaling slowing push both palm hands out to full arm extension.
15. Switch both feet in place ending in a right foot back stance, execute middle knife hand block.

16. Step forward with right foot into side stance, execute right side thrust punch.
17. Shift weight to left foot back stance, execute inside block with right fist.
18. Step forward with left foot into side stance, execute left side thrust punch.
19. Sift weight into left leg back forward stance, high knife hand block with left arm, right fist low block.
20. Step forward with right foot into forward stance, execute low block with right fist.
21. Step forward with left foot in to forward stance, execute low block with left fist.
22. Move right foot (pivoting on the left foot) Lift right foot into right leg forward stance, simultaneously extend both arms straight out away from body, left fist in front of left knee and higher, right fist over right knee.
23. Rotate waist and upper body 180° to the left side, switching arm positions.
24. Extend the right arm out to the left arm, grasp left hand's fingers at chin height.
25. Draw back into back stance left foot forward knee locked, draw both palm hands back making a scooping motion and bring both hands to lower abdomen level, palm over back of the hand, palms facing downward. While moving forward into a forward stance with left foot forward, draw both open hands up to chest level, and then exhaling slowing push both palm hands out to full arm extension.
26. Bring both palm hands back to hips, inhaling slowly, shift weight to back right leg, draw back into back stance right foot forward knee locked,
27. While moving forward into a forward stance with left foot forward, draw both open hands up to chest level, and then exhaling slowing push both palm hands out to full arm extension.
28. Draw right hand back to right hip, while pressing down with extended right palm hand, execute left leg front low thrust kick with toes pointed out to the left.
29. Step forward into left leg forward stance, simultaneously extend both arms straight out away from body, left fist in front of left knee and higher, right fist over right leg.
30. Rotate waist and upper body 180[1] to the left side.
31. Extend the left arm out to the right arm, grasp right hand's fingers at chin height.
32. Draw back into back stance left foot forward knee locked, making a scooping motion and bring both hands to lower abdomen level, palm over back of the hand, palms facing downward. While moving forward into a forward stance with left foot forward, draw both open hands up to chest level, and then exhaling slowing push both palm hands out to full arm extension.
33. Bring both palm hands back to hips, inhaling slowly, shift weight to back right leg, draw back into back stance left foot forward knee locked,

34. While moving forward into a forward stance with left foot forward, draw both open hands up to chest level, and then exhaling slowing push both palm hands out to full arm extension.
35. Draw back into back stance right foot forward, inside block with right fist.
36. Step forward with left foot into side stance, execute left side thrust punch.
37. Shift weight to right foot back, back stance, execute inside block with left fist.
38. Step forward with right foot into side stance, execute right side thrust punch.
39. Sift weight into right leg back forward stance, high knife hand block with right arm, left fist low block.
40. Step forward with left foot, forward stance, execute low block with left fist.
41. Step forward with right foot into right foot forward stance, forward punch with right fist.

Chun Bee.

YUKRO CHO DAN

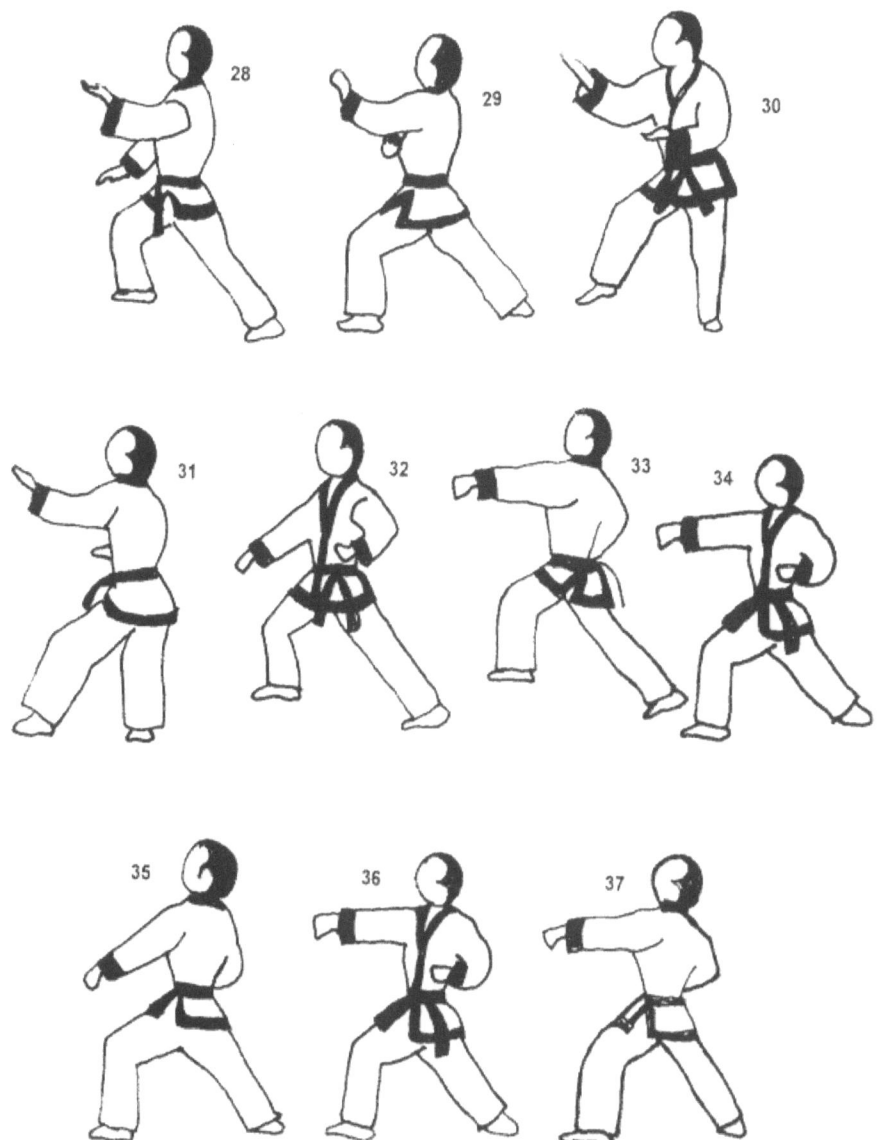

YUK RO EE DAN HYUNG

1. Chun Bee
2. Step forward with left foot into modified back stance with left foot forward, execute upper palm hand push with left hand to chest height and downward right-hand palm push to almost right knee level.
3. Step forward into left foot forward stance, execute rising palm hand push to shoulder height with right hand and lower palm hand push with left hand to waist height.
4. Step forward into forward stance with right leg forward, execute reinforced fore arm block with right fist.
5. Step forward with left foot into right leg back stance, execute lower knife hand block with left hand.
6. Step forward with right leg, left leg forward back stance, execute lower knife hand block.
7. Move your body weight to the right leg, rotate upper body 180°, execute right hand high palm hand block behind head, left palm hand facing down under right elbow.
8. Step forward with left leg into left leg forward right leg back stance, execute left hand middle knife hand block.
9. Step forward with left foot into forward stance, slowly execute simultaneous palm hand block with right hand forward to chest level, left hand to lower waist level.
10. Move weight forward onto left leg, rotate upper body 180°, left leg behind right, execute right left high palm hand block behind head, right palm hand facing down under right elbow.
11. Step forward with right foot into left leg back stance, execute middle knife hand block with right hand.
12. Step forward with right foot into forward stance, slowly execute simultaneous palm hand block with left hand forward to chest level, left hand to lower waist level.
13. Turn to the left, lower body onto fully bent right leg, left leg extends out away from right, rest on side of left foot, execute left hand lower knife hand block.
14. Shift weight to fully bent left leg, extend right leg out away from left, rest on right side of foot, execute right hand lower knife hand block.
15. Step forward with left foot into right leg back stance, execute high palm hand block over the head with right hand, open left hand to right side at waist level.
16. Step with left foot forward into side stance, execute slow simultaneous palm hand push blocks hands facing upward with extended arms to sides.
17. Bend right arm at elbow, move to in front of face.

18. Step with right foot forward into side stance, execute slow simultaneous palm hand push blocks hands facing upward with extended arms to sides.
19. Bend left arm at elbow, move to in front of face.
20. Pivot on balls of feet 90° right into a forward stance with right leg forward, execute left hand high block.
21. Execute high forward punch with right fist.
22. Execute high forward punch with left fist.
23. Move weight to right foot change into cat stance, right foot forward, reinforced forearm block with right arm.
24. Step forward left foot into forward stance, inside out block with left fist, low groin strike with knife hand to hip level, out over right knee.
25. Pivot 180o with right foot into forward stance, execute inside block with right fist, low groin knife hand with left.
26. Move weight to right foot change into cat stance, right foot forward, reinforced forearm block with right arm.
27. Shift weight forward into right foot forward stance, execute rising palm hand push to shoulder height with left hand and lower palm hand push with right hand to waist height.
28. Execute rising palm hand push to shoulder height with right hand and lower palm hand push with left hand to waist height.
29. Step forward with left foot into forward stance, execute reinforced forearm block with left arm.
30. Step forward with right foot into back stance, right foot forward, execute middle knife hand block.
31. Step backward with right foot into back stance, left leg forward, execute middle knife hand block.
32. Step forward with right leg into forward stance, execute low block with right fist.
33. Execute a reverse forward punch with left fist.
34. Execute forward punch with right fist.
35. Step forward left foot into forward stance, execute low block with left fist.
36. Execute forward punch with right fist.
37. Execute forward punch with left fist.
38. Execute hook punch with right fist, execute front thrust kick with right foot.
39. Land in forward stance with right foot forward, execute hook punch with left fist, execute front thrust kick with left foot.
40. Land forward with right foot into left leg back stance, execute high palm hand block over the head with right hand, open left hand to right side at waist level.
41. Step with right leg 180° into side stance, while pivoting on left foot, execute high blocks to both sides with both fists.
42. Execute punch over left shoulder with right fist.
43. Execute punch over right shoulder with left fist.
44. Chun Bee.

YUKRO EE DAN

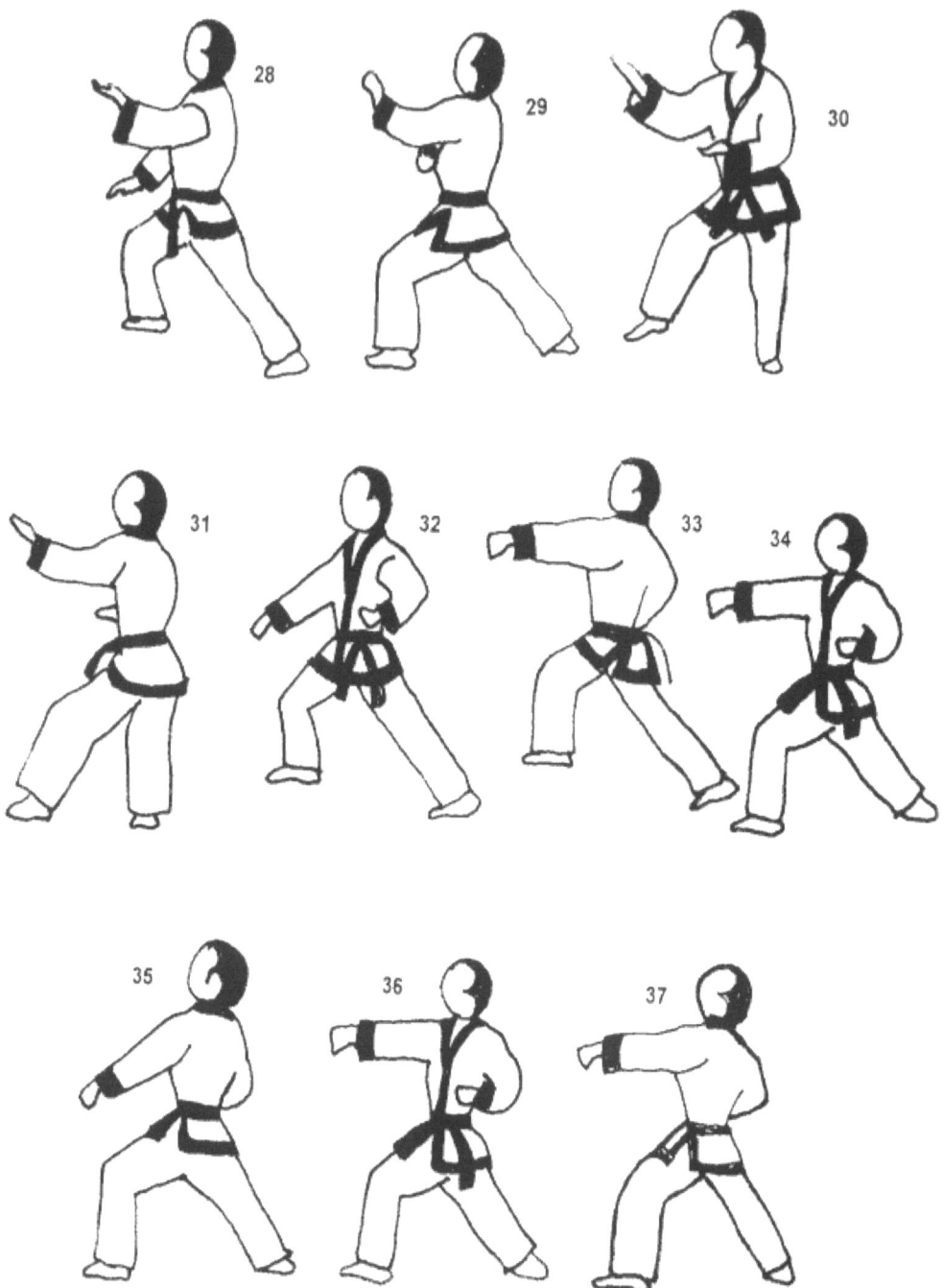

YUK RO SUM DAN HYUNG

1. Chun Bee
2. Step out and rotate body 90° with right foot into side stance, execute embracing motion with left hand high at shoulder level, right hand at stomach level.
3. Step with right foot while pivoting on the left foot 135°, execute embracing movement, right hand high at shoulder level, left hand at stomach level.
4. Step out and rotate body 90° with left foot into side stance, execute embracing motion with left hand high at shoulder level, right hand at stomach level.
5. Step forward with left foot into forward stance, outstretch both arms and fists in front and behind at shoulder level.
6. Rotate upper body and arms 180°.
7. Step forward with right foot onto forward stance while extending both arms and both fists.
8. Rotate upper body 180° to the right while changing arms and fists position.
9. Execute right hand hammer fist strike, left fist to left hip.
10. Execute left hand hammer fist strike, right fist to left hip.
11. Execute simultaneous knife hand strike, right to the front groin area, left to the rear groin area.
12. Execute a forward low knife hand strike with left hand and rear knife hand strike with the right.
13. Step forward with left foot, bring right foot behind, execute left hand back fist strike to the left, right palm hand is covering at lower right chin area.
14. Step out 90° to the right with your right foot into forward stance, execute left palm hand straight out at chest level, right low groin area knife hand strike.
15. Rotate 180° on both feet into forward stance, right palm hand at chest level, left knife hand to the rear groin area.
16. Step forward with right foot into a right foot forward stance, right fist inside block left fist to left hip.
17. Execute reverse inside out block with left fist, right fist to right hip.
18. Step forward with left foot into forward stance, left fist inside block.
19. Execute reverse inside out block with right fist, left fist to left hip.
20. Execute forward punch to the mid section.
21. Execute right fist forward punch.
22. Bring right foot while pivoting on left foot 90°, to the right foot, cross wrists at chest level, right in front of left.
23. Step with left foot 135° to the left into side stance, execute embracing movement with left arm high and right low, palm hands facing inward.

24. Step with right foot 90° to the right into side stance, execute embracing movement with left arm high and right arm low, palm hands facing inward.
25. Step forward to the right with right foot into forward stance, extend both arms out and fists out shoulder level.
26. Rotate upper body and arms 180°.
27. Step forward with right foot onto forward stance while extending both arms and both fists, left arm forward, right to the rear.
28. Rotate upper body 180° to the right while changing arms and fists position, right arm forward, left behind.
29. Execute upper block with left fist.
30. Step forward with right foot into right foot forward stance, execute a forward punch with right fist.
31. Execute reverse left fist forward punch.
32. Execute simultaneous knife hand strikes to the front and rear groin area, right hand forward, left to the rear.
33. Rotate upper body and arms 180° to the right, left hand forward, right arm back.
34. Step forward with left foot, bring right foot behind, body face to the right, face forward, execute back fist strike with the right fist shoulder height.
35. Step out to the right with right foot into forward stance, execute outstretched left palm hand to chest level, right knife to the rear for groin area strike.
36. Pivot on both feet turning 180° into a forward stance with left leg forward, execute simultaneous right palm hand push to the chest area, left knife hand strikes to the rear groin area.
37. Shift weight back to right leg into back stance, left leg forward.
38. Step forward into right leg forward stance, right forward punch, left fist to left hip.
39. Shift weight back to right leg into back stance, left leg forward, upper block with right fist.
40. Execute left arm upper block.
41. Step forward with left leg high punch with right fist.
42. Execute left fist high punch

43. Chun Bee

YUK RO SUM DAN

HWA SUN HYUNG

1. Chun Bee
2. Move left foot to right foot, while bringing both chambered fists to each side.
3. Look to the left and turn 90° degrees to the left with your left foot into a primitive front stance, grasp your left fingers with your right hand.
4. Execute scooping motion with both hands, as they arrive at the chest, shift weight into full forward stance while pushing straight out with both palm hands facing away from body.
5. Look to the right and turn 90° to the right into forward facing side stance, execute double low block with right fist and high behind the head block with left fist.
6. Look and turn 90° to the left and step forward with right foot into right foot forward stance, execute an overhead hammer fist strike.
7. Execute a reverse overhead hammer fist strike.
8. Look and turn 180° to the right 180° into a primitive forward stance with right foot forward, grasp right fingers with left hand.
9. Execute scooping motion with both hands, as they arrive at the chest, shift weight into full forward stance while pushing straight out with both palm hands facing away from body.
10. Look and turn 90° to the left into side stance, execute double low block with left fist and high behind the head with the right fist.
11. Look and turn 90°, step forward with left foot into forward stance left foot forward. Execute a left-hand overhead hammer fist strike.
12. Execute a reverse overhead hammer fist strike.
13. Look and turn 135° to the left, rotate right foot and hop forward onto the left leg, move right leg behind left at back of left knee, execute simultaneous open palm push blocks, left palm hand goes high over head, palm up, the right arm pushes straight down at groin level, palm down.
14. Hop to the rear and land on right leg with left foot behind right knee, execute double open hand blocks, the right palm hand high behind head palm hand facing back of head, left palm hand low in front of left thigh.
15. Look and step forward into primitive stance with left foot, execute simultaneous open hand block and cover, right palm hand at right shoulder height, left palm hand facing down under right palm hand.
16. Look and turn 135° to the right, hop forward onto the right leg, move left leg behind left at back of left knee, execute simultaneous open palm push blocks, left palm hand goes high over head, palm up, the right arm pushes straight down at groin level, palm down.
17. Hop forward and land on left leg with right leg behind left knee, execute double open hand blocks, left palm hand behind head, right palm to low position in front of right thigh.

18. Step forward with right foot into primitive front stance, execute simultaneous open hand block and cover, left palm hand at right shoulder height, right palm hand facing down under left palm hand and move into forward stance.
19. Step 45° to the left with left foot into forward stance, left foot forward, execute middle knife hand block in forward stance.
20. Execute front snap kick with right foot.
21. Step down with the right foot and execute a jump front snap kick with left foot. Meet left foot with left hand at kick completion.
22. Jump up with right foot and execute right foot snap kick, touch right foot with right hand when kick is completed.
23. Land in an open hand cover with right palm hand covering groin area and left palm hand covering right shoulder.
24. Step forward with your left foot into side stance, execute left hand overhead knife strike stop at shoulder height, right fist at right hip.
25. Hold palm hand extended and kick with right foot.
26. Land in forward stance with right foot forward, execute reinforced forearm block with right arm.
27. Execute simultaneous vertical knife hand strikes, right hand to the rear, left knife hand to front.
28. Execute simultaneous reverse vertical knife hand strikes, left hand to the rear, right knife hand to front.
29. Step forward with left foot into forward stance, execute simultaneous vertical knife hand strikes, right hand to the rear, left knife hand to front.
30. Execute spear hand thrust with right hand, cover with left.
31. Step out with the left foot into side stance, execute simultaneous high blocks to both right and left sides.
32. Rotate upper body 45° to the right, lower right fist to waist.
33. Rotate 90° to the right by picking up right foot, forward stance with left foot, execute left palm hand push forward, right fist at hip.
34. Rotate right fist clockwise circular motion to the side ending high and opposite right shoulder, right palm hand drooping downward.
35. Using a circular motion with right fist, slap right thigh at hip.
36. Turn 180° degrees to the left with the left foot, execute high palm hand block overhead and left palm hand to right side.
37. Turn 180° to the right by pivoting on balls of feet, into back stance, right leg forward, execute lower knife hand blocks.
38. Step forward with right foot into forward stance, execute left hand hook punch, right fist at right hip.
39. Execute left diagonal kick and land in forward stance with left leg forward.
40. Execute right fist hook punch, left fist at left hip.
41. Execute diagonal kick with right foot, land in forward stance with right foot forward.
42. Execute left hand hook punch.

43. Execute side thrust kick with left foot, land in forward stance with left foot forward.
44. Execute a right-hand hook punch.
45. Execute side thrust kick with right foot, land in back stance with right leg forward.
46. Execute middle knife hand block.
47. Step back with right foot into back stance, left foot forward, execute middle knife hand block.
48. Step forward with right foot into forward stance, right leg forward, execute forward punch with right fist.
49. Execute reverse punch with left fist.
50. Step forward with left foot into side stance, elbow strike directly in front of left side, elbow remain at 90°, right hand cover at solar plexus.
51. Step forward with right foot into side stance, right hand executes overhead knife hand strike to the right side, left fist on left hip.
52. Execute outside kick to the outstretched right palm hand, land with left foot forward.
53. Execute a left palm hand push and right-hand high knife hand block overhead.
54. Execute a right reverse palm push and a left-hand high knife hand block overhead.
55. Step forward with right foot into forward stance, execute right hammer fist strike to the front and center area, and a left hammer fist strike to the same area.
56. Execute left (going upwards) reverse hammer fist strike and a right hand (downward going) hammer fist strike.
57. Step forward with left foot into forward stance, execute rear knife strike to the groin with right knife hand, and left hand forward low knife hand strike to the front.
58. Execute rear knife strike to the groin with left knife hand, and right hand forward low knife hand strike to the front.
59. Execute left palm hand forward push, right fist to right side.
60. Switch to back stance with left leg forward, shift weight to right leg, execute low right-hand spear thrust strike, left palm hand to cover right shoulder.
61. Rise up to a back stance with right foot back, execute high right fist block and a low left block.
62. Step forward with right foot into forward stance, execute inside middle open hand area blocks.
63. Step forward with left foot into side stance, execute inside to outside high blocks.
64. Look and rotate body 45° over left shoulder, lower left arm to chest level, right arm remains high.
65. Rotate 180° using right foot into forward stance, right foot forward.
66. Right fist to right side, left knife to left side on outstretched arm.

67. Step forward with left foot, sit down with left leg extended, right leg tucked in, extend both arms out in front and to rear, left forward, right rear.
68. Stand into left foot forward front stance, execute right hand hook punch, left hand to left hip.
69. Execute front snap kick with rear right foot.
70. Land on right foot in forward stance, execute left hand hook punch, right fist to right side.
71. Execute front snap kick with rear left leg.
72. Land in left leg front stance, execute double inside out middle block.
73. Execute left palm hand pushing forward, right knife hand covers over head.
74. Execute right palm hand pushing block, left knife hand covers overhead.
75. Execute hammer fist strike going low with left fist, right hand executes hammer fist going up.
76. Execute hammer fist strike going low with right fist, left hand executes hammer fist going up.
77. Step forward into forward stance with right foot, execute reinforced forearm block with right fist.
78. Step forward with left foot into side stance, execute high inside to outside blocks.
79. Look over right shoulder and rotate body 45° over right shoulder, lower right arm to chest level, left arm remains high.
80. Rotate 180o using left foot into forward stance, left foot forward, leave left palm hand middle area.
81. Right fist to right side, left knife to left side on outstretched arm.
82. Execute center inside to outside knife hand blocks.
83. Execute right knee strike, step back into forward stance, left foot forward.
84. Execute double palm hand pushing to center area.
85. Look and turn 90° to the right with right foot into forward stance, execute right palm hand push to center area, left fist on left hip.
86. Move left arm in counter clockwise motion stopping at shoulder height, right fist to right hip.
87. Execute double inside to outside knife hand blocks.
88. Execute left knee strike.
89. Step back with left leg into forward stance, execute double palm heel pushing to center area.
90. Rotate 135° around left shoulder, stop with right leg forward, extend both arms with fists, right arm outstretched in front of right hip, left arm outstretched in front of left hip.
91. Rotate upper body 180°.
92. Rotate body 180°, right and left fist makes circular up/down motion.
93. Rotate body 180°, right and left fist makes circular up/down motion.
94. Step with right foot to make side stance, execute horizontal right elbow strike, left fist to left hip.

95. Step with left foot into forward stance outstretch both arms and fists, right arm outstretched in front of right hip, left arm outstretched in front of left hip.
96. Rotate upper body 180° to reverse position.
97. Rotate body 180°, right and left fist makes circular up/down motion.
98. Rotate body 180°, right and left fist makes circular up/down motion.
99. Step with left foot into side stance, execute horizontal elbow strike.
100. Chun Bee

HWA SUN

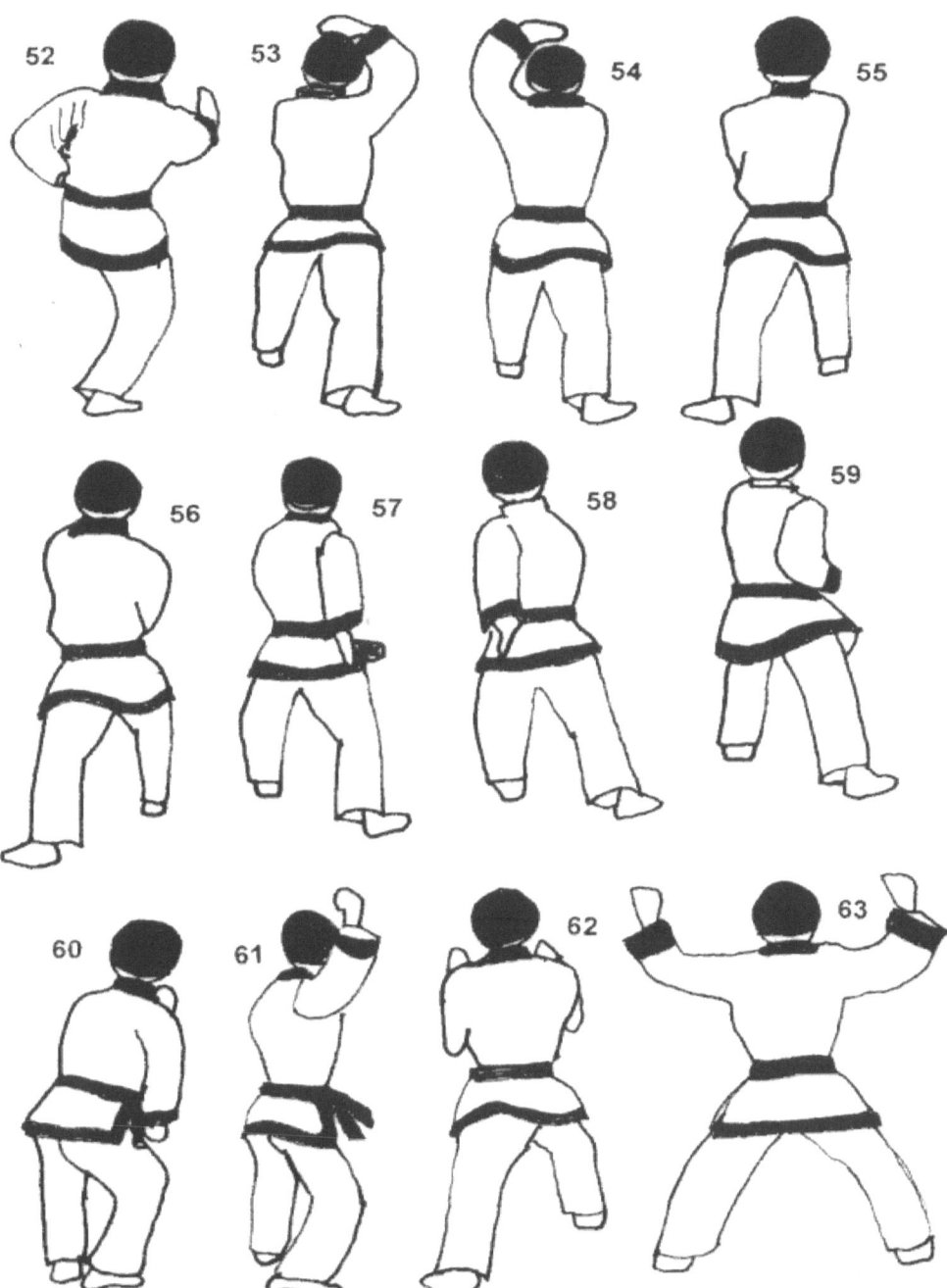

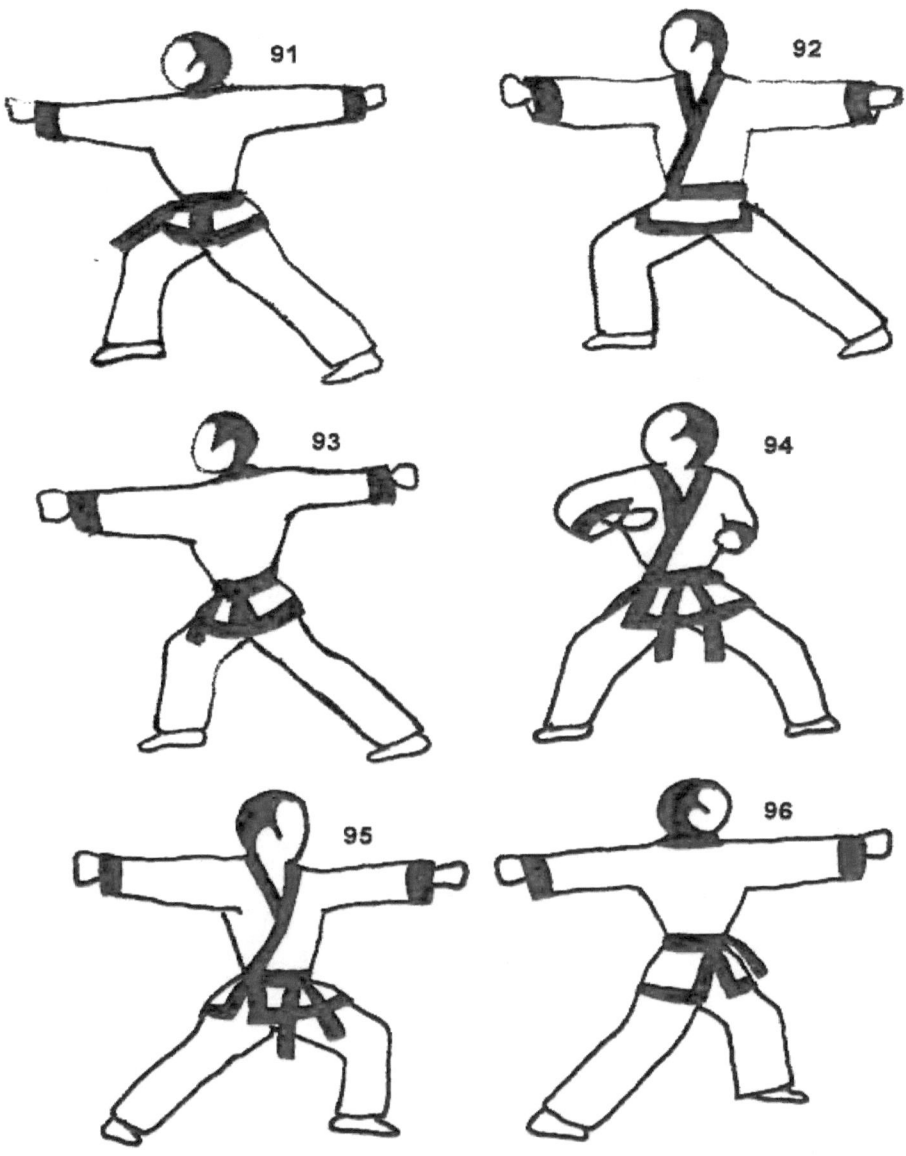

GLOSSARY

Advanced Techniques - Refers to the level of difficulty using and learning hand, foot, arm and leg self-defense and opponent control techniques. Advanced techniques are usually taught after the student learns basic and intermediate level of difficulty techniques.

Basics - Refers to the level of difficulty and order taught for the techniques and information of a style. They are usually the first things that are taught to the novice. Basics include elementary items on history, philosophy, customs, rituals, ceremonies, stances, stepping, blocks, strikes and kicks. The basics form the foundation for learning intermediate and advanced level techniques. Basics have been mistaken for the style's self defense techniques by novices. This has led to misconceptions and erroneous popular beliefs about martial arts. Basic training includes drills learned over several years for hand-eye-foot coordination and improving one's balance. These are necessary to be capable to learn the techniques at the next level.

Belt - A colored cloth belt worn around the waist identifying the wearer's level of knowledge and skill. Instructors group students based on the color of the students' belts. They select exercises and lessons on the belt color worn by the students that attend each workout. It serves as a teaching aid to the instructors, visiting instructors, and other students to quickly denote the class hierarchy.

Black Belt - A rank designating a high level of knowledge, ability and achievement. Often wearers of the black belt are instructors. Pupils look to a black belt to answer questions in a traditional class environment.

Blocking - Any technique that hinders, stops, neutralizes and nullifies an opponent's attack.

Blue Belt - A rank designating a high level of knowledge, ability and achievement in the Tang Soo Do Soo Bahk Do® Moo Duk Kwan. Often wearers of the blue belt are instructors. Pupils look to a blue belt to answer questions in a traditional class environment.

Bow - A bending of the head, shoulders or body used as a greeting or acknowledgment of position or rank.

Breaking - Smashing, striking, punching and kicking bricks, boards, concrete slabs, ice blocks or rocks to demonstrate correct power, speed, and control.

Bubishi – A book whose origin can be traced to China's Fukian province. It contains 32 articles on Bai He and Luohan Quan techniques, strategy, philosophy, vital point striking and herbal medicine.

Budoka – A person studying martial arts or martial ways.

Buddhism - An Eastern philosophy, often mistakenly referred to as a religious doctrine. It provides writings and teachings to help one become more aware and in tune with the world and be in a more harmonious state.

Ccerium - A Korean form of wrestling, similar to Japanese Sumo.

Cho (So) - Least high, lesser one, of lower importance.

Confucius - An ancient Eastern philosophy, often erroneously referred to as a religion, based on the teaching of a Chinese intellectual of the same name.

Dai (Dae) - Greatest, largest, most important.

Da Mo – Bodhidharma, an Indian prince and Buddhist monk. He is credited with the introduction of Chan (Zen) philosophy to China. It is legendary that he went to the Shaolin Temple around 520 ADE and introduced a series of exercises known as the Shiba Luohan Shou. These are used to help the monks stay awake during the meditation sessions required. He is also purported to be the founder of two styles, the Xi Sui Jing and Yi Ji Jing (which may be the same style).

Do - In Chinese, the concept of "do" is expressed as Tao, or the way, as in pathway, coarse to travel, way in which to live, and lifestyle. It is dynamic in nature, likened to a river. When 'do' is attached as a suffix, it adds this philosophical connection to the martial art, such as Karate-Do, Tae Kwon-Do, Soo Bahk-Do, Tang Soo -Do, Ju-do and Aki-Do.

Dojang - The building or room where instructors teach Korean martial arts.

Dojo - The place where instructors teach Japanese martial arts.

Form - A sequence of movements using all parts of the body. They include stepping, turning, punching, kicking, striking, jumping, hopping, rolling and bending over. Teachers use forms to demonstrate individual techniques of a style. The forms hold a style's techniques.

Funakoshi, Gichin – An Okinawa Shuri-te Instructor who moved from

Okinawa to mainland Japan in 1917. The first known Okinawa Instructor to teach Okinawa karate do in Japan. He did so at the Kyuoto Butokuden.

Gak Jeo Chong – A tomb in Manchuria that contains wall paintings of men in martial poses created by Korean artists when the Koguryo dynasty ruled the region.

Ha - The 'Ha' denotes a subgroup of the 'Ryu' and also shares a translation to the previous water analogy. If 'Do' is the river, 'Ryu' is a current and 'Ha' is an eddy associated with a current.

Instructor - An individual that has reached a high level of ability and knowledge and teaches martial arts.

Itosu, Ankoh – An Instructor of Shuri-te who studied under Matsumura Soken.

Ju Jitsu - A style of Japanese martial art whose techniques are used in almost all other styles of traditional martial arts. Judo, a martial sport and one of the Olympic games, uses a subset of techniques from Ju Jitsu.

Kai - The 'Kai' can be a meeting, an assembly, party, association, club or society. Members use the 'Kai' to organize agreed upon policies, procedures and principles.

Kan - A place usually taken to mean a hall, building, gymnasium or special meeting place.

Kendo - A sword art and sport, identical to Korean Kumdo.

Kick - An offensive technique that uses the leg and foot to inflict pain.

Kuen - The term used to denote the forms of kung fu styles (See form).

Kumdo - A sword art and sport identical to Japanese Kendo

Kwan/Kan/Kwoon - A place usually taken to mean a hall, building, gymnasium or special meeting place.

Kwon Bup Bu – (Fist Method Steps) An ancient martial art described in the text of the *Moo Yei Do Bo Tong Ji.* Very little is known about this style.

Kyudo - The study of sport Japanese archery with the philosophical principles of Zen Buddhism. Kyudo evolved from kyujutsu after firearms were introduced to Japan.

Kyujutsu - The name given to classical combat archery of the Japanese feudal era.

Martial Art - A term used to describe well organized, well structured, well-disciplined regimen of training, philosophy and self-defense practices. The primary focus is the student's development through internal awareness training and intense physical self-defense training (see fighting art).

Meibuken – (Enlightened Martial Fist) The name of the school used by Yagi Meitoku to refer to the fighting applications taught.

Master - A high level of instructor.

Punch - A strike using the first set of large knuckles of the hand.

Rank - A style will include levels of skill and experience. The rank brackets the difficulty level of the training for a practitioner during a work-out.

Ryu - Ryu is like "Do" When a word has 'Ryu' attached, it denotes a sub-relationship with the greater 'Do'. Both are dynamic in nature, much as a current in a river, where the 'Ryu' is the current and the 'Do' is the river.

School - The style, location, building, system and the instructor of martial arts.

So - See Cho

Strike - Any of the offensive techniques used by the upper body such as hands, arms, head and elbows.

Style - The components of a martial art system, that take on qualities of an instructor.

Sumo - A Japanese competition using a style of wrestling similar to Korean, Serium.

System - The components that include: offensive and defensive striking and blocking techniques, stances and maneuvers, forms, philosophy, customs, ceremonies, rituals and doctrine.

BIBLIOGRAPHY

Losik, Len, *Tang Soo Do, A Korean Martial Art, Question and Answer Book*, SanLen Publishing, Maineville, Ohio.

Losik, Len, *Parent's Guide to Children's Martial Arts*, SanLen Publishing, Maineville Ohio.

Losik, Len, *A History of Tang Soo Do*, World of Martial Arts, June 1998, Pacific Rim Publishing, Santa Clara, California.

Losik, Len, *Secrets of the Asian Masters*, SanLen Publishing, 1999, Folsom, CA

Losik, Len, *The Resurrection of Subahk*, World of Martial Arts, March/April 1997, Pacific Rim Publishing, Santa Clara California.

Losik, Len, *Too Many Tae Kwon Do Hyung?* Mudo Dojang, October, 1995, Pacific Rim Publishing, Santa Clara California.

Losik, Len, *Tae Kwon Do: Korea's 20th Century Mirror*, Tae Kwon Do Times, July, 1995. Tri-Mount Publications, Bettendorf, Iowa.

Losik, Len, *Ground Zero: How the Atomic Bomb and its Aftermath Brought the Asian Martial Arts To The Modern World, Part I,* Inside Tae Kwon Do, CFW Enterprises, Burbank California, December, 1995.

Losik, Len, *Ground Zero: How the Atomic Bomb and its Aftermath Brought the Asian Martial Arts To The Modern World, Part II,* Inside Tae Kwon Do, CFW Enterprises, Burbank California, January, 1996.

Losik, Len, *Classical Hyung of Korea*, Tae Kwon Do Times, March, 1998. Tri-Mount Publications, Bettendorf, Iowa.

Losik, Len, *Healing Power of Tae Kwon Do*, World of Martial Arts, June 1996, Pacific Rim Publishing, Santa Clara, California.

Losik, Len, *Is Tae Kwon Do a System or a Style?* World of Martial Arts, June 1995, Pacific Rim Publishing, Santa Clara, California.

Hans Biedermann, Dictionary of Symbolism, Cultural Icons & the Meanings Behind Them, 1992, Penguin Book Publishing, 375 Hudson Street, New York New York.

Hood, John, *Chang Ch'ien's Far Reaching Diplomacy Laid the*

Groundwork for Han Conquest-and the Link Between East and West. Military History, April, 1996, Military History, Leesburg, Virginia.

Summers, Harry, G. *The Korean War, A Fresh Perspective*, Military History, April, 1996, Military History, Leesburg, Virginia.

Haydock, Michael D, *America's Other Korean War*, Military History, April, 1996, Military History, Leesburg, Virginia.

Cohen, Theodore, *Remaking Japan*, The Free Press, New York.

Losik, Len, *Moo Duk Kwan, Miracle or Mistake?* Tae Kwon Do Times, September, 1997. Tri-Mount Publications, Bettendorf, Iowa.

Losik, Len, *Tae Kwon Do Meditation?* Mudo Dojang, April, 1996, Pacific Rim Publishing, Santa Clara California.

Losik, Len, *Merging of the Martial Arts Organizations, Myth or Miracle?* Tae Kwon Do Times, July, 1995. Tri-Mount Publications, Bettendorf, Iowa.

Streep, Peg, *Confucius The Wisdom,* A Bulfinch Press Book, Little, Brown and Company, New York, USA.

Tomio, Nagaboshi, *The Bodhisattva Warriors*, Samuel Weiser, Inc., York Beach, ME.

Kim, He-Young, *General Choi Hong Hi A Tae Kwon Do History Lesson:* Tae Kwon Do Times, January, 2000. Tri-Mount Publications, Bettendorf, Iowa.

Kee, Hwang, *Tang Soo Do (Soo Bahk Do)*, Copyright 1978, Korean Soo Bahk Do Association, Seoul, Korea.

Losik, Len, A History of Tang Soo Do, World of Martial Arts, June 1998, Pacific Rim Publishing, Santa Clara, California.

Kee, Hwang, *The History of the Moo Duk Kwan*, US Tang Soo Do Moo Duk Kwan Federation, Springfield, New Jersey.

Losik, Len, *The Chang Moo Kwan: WTF's foundation*, Tae Kwon Do Times, July, 2000. Tri-Mount Publications, Bettendorf, Iowa.

Draeger, Donn F., and Robert W. Smith, *Comprehensive Asian Fighting Arts*, Kadansha International, Tokyo, Japan.

Losik, Len, *East Meets West*, Losik, Len, *Tae Kwon Do:* Tae Kwon Do Times, November, 1998. Tri-Mount Publications, Bettendorf, Iowa.

Funakoshi, Gichin, *Karate-Do Nyumon, The Masters Text*, Kadansha International, Tokyo, Japan.

Losik, Len Endangered *Species, Tae Kwon Do's Animal Hyung*, World of Martial Arts, January 1996, Pacific Rim Publishing, Santa Clara, California.

Funakoshi, Gichin, *Karate-Do Kyohan, The Masters Text*, Kadansha International, Tokyo, Japan.

Losik, Len, *Little Known Kwans of Korea*, Tae Kwon Do Times, March, 2002, Tri-Mount Publications, Bettendorf, Iowa.

Nakayama, M., *Best Karate, Vol 1 thru Vol 11,* Kadansha International, Tokyo, Japan.

Losik, Len, *Tae Kwon Do: A Bumpy Ride to Sydney,* Tae Kwon Do Times, October, 1996. Tri-Mount Publications, Bettendorf, Iowa.

Bishop, Mark, *Okinawan Karate, Teachers, Styles and Secret Techniques,* A&C Black Limited, London, England.

Higaonna, Morio, *Traditional Karate Do, Fundamental Techniques, Vol 1 thru Vol 4,* Minato Research/Japan Publications, Japan.

Koenosuke, Enoeda, *SHOTOKAN Advanced Kata, Vol 1 thru 3,* Dragon Books, Los Angeles, California, USA.

Nagamine, Shoshine, *The Essence of Okinawa Karate-Do,* Charles E. Tuttle, Rutland, Vermont, USA.

Nakamura, Tadashi, *Karate Technique and Spirit,* Shufunotomo Co. Ltd., Tokyo, Japan.

Corcoran, John, *The Martial Arts Source Book*, Harper Perennial, New York, New York, USA.

Corcoran, John & Farkas, Emil, *The Original Martial Arts Encyclopedia, Tradition-History-Pioneers*, Pro-Action Publishing, Los Angeles, California, USA

Yang, Jwing-Ming, Ph.D., *The Essence of Shaolin White Crane Martial Power and Qigong*, YMAA Publication Center, Jamaica Plain, Massachusetts, USA.

Choi, Hong Hi, *Tae Kwon Do, The Art of Self Defence*, Daeha Publications Company, Seoul Korea.

Tohei, Koichi, *Ki In Daily Life*, Ki No Kenkyukai H.Q., Tokyo, Japan.

Kim, Young-sam, *Kim Young-sam and the New Korea*, Bonus Books, Inc., Chicago.

Chapman, William, *Inventing Japan*, Prentis Hall, New York.

Corcoran, John, Farkas, Emil, *The Overlook Martial Arts Dictionary*, The Overlook Press, New York.

Byong-Hwa, Han, *The Book on Korean Studies*, Yekyong Publications Company, Ltd, Seoul Korea.

Lee, Ki-baik, *A New History of Korea*, Seoul Korea.

Lee, Peter, H. Editor, *A Sourcebook of Korean History,* Seoul Korea.

Lee, Peter, H. an *Anthology of Korean Literature*, Seoul Korea.

The Korea Studies, University of California, Berkeley, California.

Sang Kyu Shim, *Understanding the Spirit of Tae Kwon Do Tae Kwon Do Through the History of Korea*, Tae Kwon Do Times, May 1998, Tri-Mount Publications, Bettendorf, Iowa.

Murgado, Amoury, *Yudo A Korean Martial Art for the Millennium,* Kung Fu Presents The World of Martial Arts, February, 1999, Pacific Rim Publishing, Santa Clara California.

Hwang Kee, *Tang Soo Do Soo Bahk Do Moo Duk Kwan Volume 2,* United States Soo Bahk Do® Moo Duk Kwan Federation, Inc. Springfield New Jersey.

Losik, Len, *Ji Do Kwan, Way of Wisdom*, Tae Kwon Do Times, May, 2001. Tri-Mount Publications, Bettendorf, Iowa.

Hwang Kee, *The History of Moo Duk Kwan,* 1995, United States Soo Bahk Do Moo Duk Kwan Federation, Inc. Springfield New Jersey.

Losik, Len *Tang Soo Do Korean Empty Hand Self-Defense Book of Hyung*, SanLen Publishing, Aptos, California.

Losik, Len *Tang Soo Do Korean Empty Hand Self-Defense Book of Hyung, Volume I*, SanLen Publishing, Aptos, California.

Losik, Len *Tang Soo Do Korean Empty Hand Self-Defense Book of Hyung, Volume II*, SanLen Publishing, Aptos, California.

Losik, Len *Tang Soo Do Korean Empty Hand Self-Defense Book of Hyung, Volume III*, SanLen Publishing, Aptos, California.

Hwang Kee, *Gup Level Instructional Guides*, 1993, United States Soo Bahk Do Moo Duk Kwan Federation, Inc., Springfield New Jersey.

Lee, Uk Kang, *Tang Soo Do. The Ultimate Guide to the Korean Martial Art*, 1999, A&C Black, London, England.

Choi Hong Hi, *Tae Kwon Do The Art of Self Defense,* 1963, Daeha Publications, Seoul Korea.

Sang H. Kim, The Comprehensive Illustrated Manual of Martial Arts (*Moo Yei Do Bo Tong Ji*) of Ancient Korea, 2000, Turtle Press, Hartford Connecticut.

The Ancestry of the Mongols, www.athome.powertech.no/pioe/ancestry.htm 1999.

The Analects of Confucius, 1998, www.human.toyogakuen-u.ac.jp/~acmuller/contao/analects.htm.

The Korean History Project, www.koreanhistoryproject.org.

Ueshiba, Morihei, *The Art of Peace*, Translated by John Stevens, 1992, Shambala, Boston, Massachusetts.

Lehrer, Brian, *The Korean Americans*, Harvard University Graduate School of Education, 1996, Chelsea House Publishers, New York, New York.

Losik, Len, *The Animals of Tae Kwon Do,* Tae Kwon Do Times, November, 1999, Tri-Mount Publications, Bettendorf, Iowa.

Hwang Kee, *Tang Soo Do Soo Bahk Do Moo Duk Kwan*, Volume 2,

1992, Tang Soo Do Moo Duk Kwan HQ, P.O. Box 154, Springfield, New Jersey.

Losik, Len, *A History of Tang Soo Do*, World of Martial Arts, June 1998, Pacific Rim Publishing, Santa Clara, California.

Kang Seok Lee, Grandmaster Won Kuk Lee Founder of Chung Do Kwan, March, 1997, Tae kwon Do Times Magazine, Tri-Mount Publications, Bettendorf, Iowa.

Weiss, Earl, Nam Tae Hi Chung Do Kwan's Quiet Man, Jan 2000, Tri Mount Press, Bettendorf, Iowa.

Losik, Len, The History of the Song Moo Kwan, Tae Kwon Do Times, May, 1999, Trimount Publications, Bettendorf, Iowa.

Dr. Yang, Jwing-Ming, The Essence of Shaolin White Crane Martial Power and Qigong, 1996, YMAA Publication Center, Jamaica Plains, MA.

Chun, Richard, Moo Duk Kwan Tae Kwon Do, Volume 1, 1975, Ohara Publications Incorporated, Santa Clarita, California.

Chun, Richard, Moo Duk Kwan Tae Kwon Do, Volume 2, 1983, Ohara Publications Incorporated, Santa Clarita, California.

Losik, Len, The Kwans of Tang Soo Do, 2002, SanLen Publishing, Aptos, CA.

Madis, Eric. The Evolution of Tae Kwon Do from Japanese karate, Seattle, Washington.

The Shotokan Planet: www.24fightingchickens.com

Modern History of Tae Kwon Do: www.martialartsresource.com

Classic Martial Arts: www.classicmartialarts.com

Chang Moo Kwan, www.daehan-taekwondo.com

The MIT Tae Kwon Do Club: web.mit.edu.tkd

Tae Kwon Do History, www.yleesmartialarts.com

Moo Duk Kwan Tang Soo Do: www.warrior-scholar.com

US Moo Duk Kwan Federation: www.moodukkwan.org

Tang Soo Do discussion Board: pluto.beseen.com

http://sataekwondo.8m.com/cheongwon.htm

http://www.geocities.com/Colosseum/Loge/8122/Hyung.htm

http://fbcsaks.org/ministries/kidokyo/faith.htmlmh

SanLen Publishing, Books and Articles by Len Losik: www.homestead.com/sanlen1

Many other internet web sites too numerous to mention.

INDEX

A

advanced á 123
advanced technique á 123
ancient á 124
animal Hyung á 18, 43, 44, 48
Archeologists á 30
Arizona á 35
art á 129
Asia á 127, 128
Asian á 125

B

balance á 123
basic á 123
basics á 123
Bassai á 49
bear á 44, 46, 48
belt á 123
Belt á 123
Bibliography á 13, 127
Big Dipper á 43, 45, 46
Black Belt á 30, 41, 123
blocking á 123
Book of Martial Arts with Illustrations á 27
Book of Martial Text with Illustrations á 28
Book of Military Preparations á 27
Bruce Lee á 35
Buddhism á 123, 124, 125
Buddhist á 24
bull á 48
Bull á 49
Byung Bup Daeji á 27
Byung Jik Ro á 29
Byungjang Dosul á 27

C

Canada á 41
ceremonies á 123, 126
Cerium á 124, 126
Chang á 30, 46, 127, 128, 131
Chang Moo Kwan á 30
Chang Moo Kwan á 35, 39
Chil Sung á 18, 43, 45, 46
Chil Sung Hyung á 45, 46
China á 30, 31
Chinese á 124
Chinto á 49
Choi á 31, 32, 34, 35
Choi Hong Hi á 31, 32, 34
Choi, Hong Hi á 129
Chosan Yen Moo Kwan á 41
Chosan Yun Moo Kwan á 41
Chuan Fa á 19, 44, 47, 48
Chun á 41
Chun Chu á 18, 21
Chun, Sang Sup á 30, 31, 41
Chung Do Kwan á 29, 30, 33, 34, 36, 37, 38, 39, 131
Chung Sun Kang á 35
clan á 30
class á 123, 125
Cobra á 49
Comprehensive Book of Military Tactics á 27
Comprehensive Illustrations of Military Generals á 28
Comprehensive Military Chronicle of the Eastern Kingdom á 27
Confucian philosophy á 28
Confucius á 124, 128, 130
coup á 22
crane á 44, 48
Crane á 129

D

Dae Han Soo Bahk Hoi á 22
David Zanger á 35
defense á 125
Do á 124
dojang á 30, 41
Dojang á 124
Dojo á 124
Dong Kuk University á 34
Dongkuk Byungkam á 27
Dr. Shin á 41
dragon á 48
drills á 123

E

eagle á 44, 48
Eastern á 123, 124

Empi á 49
England á 129

F

Five Element á 48
Five Element system á 48
forms á 124, 125, 126
Forms á 124
Funakoshi Ginchin á 45

G

Gang Duk Kwan á 41
Gankaku á 49
General Choi á 32, 34, 128
Germany á 30
Ginto á 48
Glossary á 13, 123
Gojushiho á 49
GrandMaster Hwang Kee á 17, 18, 19, 29, 43, 47, 49

H

Ha á 124
Han á 127, 129
Han Dynasty á 18
Han Kyo á 27
Han Moo Kwan á 33, 37, 38, 40
Han Moo Kwan Kwan Bup Bu á 40
Han Moo Kwan Tae Kwon Do á 40
Han Seo á 18
Han Su á 21
Handbook of Military Commanding for Generals á 28
Hangetsu á 49
Hapkido á 40
hawk á 48
Heron á 49
history á 123
History á 129
Ho Sun Kang á 35
hopping á 124
Hwa Rang á 41
Hwa Soo á 30, 32
Hwa Soo Do á 30, 31, 32
Hwa Sun á 18, 43, 47
HWA SUN á 105, 109
Hwa Sung á 47

Hwang Kee á 17, 18, 19, 21, 22, 29, 30, 31, 32, 43, 44, 45, 46, 47, 48, 130, 131
Hwarang á 31
Hyun Rung Ji á 21
Hyung á 47

I

ice-age á 30
imagineau line á 27
Imperial military á 30
Inchon á 34
include Anthony D'Amico á 35
institute of knowledge á 41
instructor á 123, 124, 125, 126
Instructor á 123, 124
instructors á 123, 124
intermediate á 123
ITF á 34, 35

J

Jangphillam Hunyung Charok á 28
Japan á 30, 31, 41, 128, 129
Japanese á 17, 18, 22, 30, 31, 48, 124, 125, 126
Japanese Masters á 30
Japan's occupation á 30
Ji Do Kwan á 40, 41
Jion á 44, 48, 49
Ju Jitsu á 124
Judo á 40, 41, 124
jumping á 124
Jung Do Kwan á 33, 36, 37
Jutte á 49

K

Kai á 125
Kan á 125, 131
Kang Duk Kwan á 33, 35
Kang Sang Koon á 49
Kang, Suh Chong á 30
Kanku á 49
Kara á 31, 32, 41
Karate á 30, 31, 35, 40, 124, 128, 129
Karate Do á 31, 32
Kee Cho Hyung á 44, 46
Kee, Hwang á 30, 128
Kendo á 40, 125
Khitanese á 21

Ki á 129
kick á 125
kicking á 124
King Jungjo á 28
King Munjong á 27
King Sado á 28
King Se Jo á 21
King Sejo á 27
Koguryo á 21
Kong Sang Koon á 44, 48
Kong Soo á 41
Kong Soo Do á 40, 41
Kook Sul á 31
Korea á 22, 29, 30, 31, 32, 33, 34, 40, 41, 127, 128, 129, 130, 143
Korean civilization á 30
Korean culture á 31
Korean Hand Strike Way Association á 22
Kor-yo á 21
Kuem á 18, 43, 46, 47
kuen á 125
Kuk Moo Kwan á 30, 33, 34, 35
Kuk Moo Kwan Tang Soo Do á 33, 34
Kuk Mu Kwan Tae Kwon Do á 34
Kuk Mu Kwan Tang Soo Do á 34
Kumdo á 21, 40, 41, 125
Kung Fu á 125, 130
Kusanku á 49
Kwan á 7, 22, 29, 30, 32, 40, 41, 125, 128, 131
Kwan Bup Bu á 41
Kwan/Kan á 125
Kwans á 40, 41
Kwon Bup á 17, 18, 19, 30, 31, 35, 39, 40, 41, 43, 45, 46, 125
Kwon Bup Bu á 31, 40, 41
kwoon á 125
Kyudo á 125
kyujutsu á 125
Kyukoshinkai á 35

L

land á 129
Lee Duk Moo á 43, 46
Lee, Byung In á 41
Lee, Kyo Yoon á 40
Lee, Kyo-Yoon á 41
Lee, Kyung Suk á 40, 41
lessons á 123
library á 18, 27, 32

M

Manchuria á 18
mantis á 48
Mao Yuanyi á 28
martial art á 125
martial arts á 22, 30, 32, 124, 125
Master á 125, 128
Master Hwang Kee á 22, 29, 30, 32
Master Itosu á 44, 45
Ming á 129
MIT á 35
Mo Eui Won á 27
Mongol á 21, 130
Moo Bee Ji á 27
Moo Duk Kwan á 9, 17, 18, 19, 22, 23, 24, 25, 26, 29, 30, 31, 32, 33, 38, 43, 44, 45, 48, 49, 128, 130, 131, 132
Moo Duk Kwan Soo Bahk Do á 17, 18, 29
Moo Duk Kwan Soo Bahk. Tang Soo Do á 18
Moo Duk Kwan Tang Soo Do á 17, 18, 19, 22, 29, 31, 32, 45, 48, 49, 132
Moo Duk Kwan Tang Soo Do Soo Bahk á 18, 32
Moo Duk Kwan Tang Soo Do Soo Bahk Do® á 18
Moo Ye Je Bo á 27, 28
Moo Ye Shin Bo á 28
Moo Yei Do Tong Bo Ji á 22
Moo Yei Tong Bo Ji á 17, 18, 22, 32
movements á 124

N

Na Ha á 48, 51
Nai Hanji á 13, 44, 48, 49, 51
NAI HANJI E DAN á 73
NAI HANJI SUM DAN á 77
Nam Tae Hi á 31
New Book of Martial Text and Illustrations á 28
North star á 45
novice á 123

O

O Do Kwan á 31, 33, 35, 37, 38
O Do Kwan Tang Soo Do á 31
O Sip Sa Bo á 48, 49

Okinawa á 129
Okinawan á 31, 32
Okinawan arts á 18
Okinawan culture á 18
Okinawan Karate Do á 18, 31, 36, 38, 39, 48, 124
Olympic á 124
original nine Kwans á 40

P

Paek Dong-su á 28
Paekche á 21
Pak Jae-ga á 28
Passai á 48, 49
Preying Mantis á 48, 49
Prince Se Ja Se Do á 28
punching á 124
Pusan á 41
Pyung Ahn Hyung á 44, 45, 46, 51
PYUNG AHN O DAN á 69
PYUNG AHN SA DAN á 65
PYUNG AHN SUM DAN á 61

Q

Qi Ji Kwang á 28

R

Rank á 125
rat á 128, 129, 130
Raul Acevedo á 35
Ro á 128
Rohai á 49
Royal Library á 28
Ryu á 125

S

school á 125
self-defense á 125
Seoul á 17, 18, 23, 32, 34, 35, 36, 37, 38, 39, 40, 41, 128, 129, 130
Seoul railroad yard library á 17
seven stars á 43, 45, 46
Shaolin á 129, 131
Ship Dan Kuem á 18, 47
Ship Dan Kyum á 43

Ship Sam á 44
Ship Soo á 48
Ship Sum á 48
Shotokan á 30
Silla Dynasty á 21
Sip Dan Kuem á 47
Sip Pal Kî á 21
Sip Soo á 49
snake á 48
So Gong Dong á 41
Sochin á 49
Sojin á 48, 49
Sok Byungjang Dosuk á 28
Song Moo Kwan á 29, 30, 31, 33, 39, 131
Song Moo Kwan Tae Kwon Do á 29
Song Moo Kwan Tang Soo Do á 29, 31
Soo Bahk á 1, 3, 4, 5, 7, 13, 17, 18, 19, 21, 22, 26, 28, 29, 31, 32, 33, 39, 40, 43, 44, 45, 47, 48, 49, 51, 124, 128, 130, 131, 143
Soo Bahk Do á 22
Soo Bahk Do Association á 128
SOO BAHK HYUNG á 51
South Korea á 29, 40
speed á 123
stances á 123, 126
strike á 126
striking á 123, 124, 126
student á 123
students á 123
study á 125
style á 123, 124, 125, 126
Subahk á 41, 127
Suh Chong Kang á 33, 34
Suk Chong Kang á 33
Sumo á 126
Sung Dynasty á 48
swallow á 44, 48
Swallow á 49
system á 126

T

Tae Kwon á 129
Tae Kwon Do á 17, 26, 29, 31, 32, 34, 35, 37, 38, 39, 40, 41, 127, 128, 129, 130, 131, 132
Tae Kyon á 41
Tae Kyun á 17, 21, 41, 43
Tae Soo Do á 31, 32, 40
Tang Soo á 29, 30, 32, 127, 128
Tang Soo Do á 17, 18, 22, 25, 26, 29, 30, 31, 32, 33, 34, 36, 37, 38, 39, 44, 49, 127, 128, 130, 131, 132, 143

Tang Soo Do (Soo Bahk Do) á 22
Tang Soo Do Kwans á 33
Tang Soo Do Moo Duk Kwan á 17, 22, 44, 131
Taoism á 124
teach á 123, 124
technique á 7, 123, 124, 125, 126
techniques á 123, 124, 125
terrible hand á 17, 18
the *Moo Yei Do Bo Tong Ji* á 19, 22, 32
three kingdoms á 21
tiger á 44, 48
Tiger á 49
Tjin á 44, 49
Tokyo á 30, 128, 129
traditional á 123, 124
Traditional á 129
training á 7, 123
Twelve Animal á 48
Twelve Animal system á 48

U

Un Su á 49
United States á 34, 40
upper body á 126
Ursa Major á 46
US á 128, 129
Useishi á 49

W

Wa á 30, 40, 41
Wang Kon á 21

Wang Shu á 48
Wangshu á 49
Wanshu á 49
Wei á 128
Won Kuk Lee á 30, 31, 32, 34, 131
Woon Su á 49
World War II á 18, 21, 24, 25, 30, 33, 35, 36
wrestling á 124, 126
WW II á 30

X

Xin Yi Liu He Quan á 48
Xing Yi Quan á 48

Y

Yakov Royter á 35
Yi Dok-mu á 28
Yi Dynasty á 21, 28, 46
Yi family á 27, 28
YMCA á 41
YMCA Kwon Bup á 41
Young Soo Ha á 35
Yudo á 40, 41
Yuk Ro á 13, 18, 43, 46, 51
YUK RO CHO DAN HYUNG á 81
YUK RO E DAN HYUNG á 89
YUK RO SUM DAN HYUNG á 97
Yun Moo Kwan á 30, 31, 33, 37, 39, 41
Yun Moo Kwan Bup Bu á 41
Yun, Byung In á 30

ABOUT THE AUTHOR:

The author lives and trains in California. He earned 5th Dan Black Belts in Tang Soo Do and Tae Kwon Do almost simultaneously followed by a 3rd Dan in Soo Bahk. The author is married and is a father of three children and five grandchildren.

The author has trained in boxing while in college and organized martial arts since 1976 when he joined his first Tae Kwon Do class after graduating from college the first time.

The author began teaching martial arts in 1983 and used aspects of martial arts in his personal life for more than 25 years to bring order, wisdom, patience, understanding and self-awareness.

Len augments his martial arts with Zen, weight training, hand speed bag, heavy bag and long-distance running. Meditation helps keep his body-mind-spirit healthy and in-tack allowing Len to train at higher levels of performance while minimizing injuries.

The author has written and has published many magazine articles and books, writing extensively about Korean martial arts. He has written and published more than 20 martial arts magazine articles for magazines including the prestigious *Mudo Dojang*, *Tae Kwon Do Times* and *Black Belt*.

Many of the author's articles illustrate the forgotten history and evolution of Korean martial arts. For this reason, Len's articles are often republished because of their excellent historical content, unavailable otherwise. Len's articles also appear on many martial arts web sites around the world.

The author's books include the traditional styles of Tang Soo Do, Soo Bahk and Tae Kwon Do Korean martial arts. Len's books and articles have been translated into many languages and one book received the Good Housekeeping Seal of Approval. The author has more than 28 years of martial arts experience.

Len has earned 5th Dan Black Belt in Moo Duk Kwan Tang Soo Do and Moo Duk Kwan Tae Kwon Do almost simultaneously and a 3rd Dan Black

Belt in Soo Bahk.

Academically, Len has earned degrees in Physics, Mathematics, Education and Electrical Engineering and has worked professionally as a Physicist, Mechanical Engineer, Electrical Engineer and as an aerospace industry executive at several major aerospace and defense companies and telecommunications companies, and as a consultant to both NASA and the U.S. Air Force on the United States major space programs and continued as a guest lecturer at the Naval Post Graduate School in Monterey California.

Books Published by the Author:

- Tang Soo Do A Korean Martial Art Question & Answer Book
- Parent's Guide to Children's Martial Arts
- Tang Soo Do Book of Hyung Volume I
- Tang Soo Do Book of Hyung Volume II
- Tang Soo Do Book of Hyung Volume III
- Tang Soo Do Complete Set of Hyung
- Secrets of the Asian Masters
- Tang Soo Do A New Look at Old Traditions
- Tae Kwon Do The Creation, History and Evolution
- Tang Soo Do The Complete Story
- Soo Bahk Ancient Ways Modern Art Volume I
- Soo Bahk Ancient Ways Modern Art Volume II
- The Greatest People of Tang Soo Do
- The Kwans of Tang Soo Do
- The Zen Primer
- Tao Te Ching The Way of Power
- Moo Duk Kwan The History and Evolution
- Chung Do Kwan Tae Kwon Do The History and Evolution
- O Do Kwan
- Kong Soo Do
- Song Moo Kwan
- Ji Do Kwan
- Kwon Bup
- Confucius' Analects, A Western Interpretation
- The Original Five Kwans of Korean Martial Arts

www.ingramcontent.com/pod-product-compliance
Lightning Source LLC
Chambersburg PA
CBHW040911020526
44116CB00026B/27